The Buckeye Rovers in the GOLD RUSH

THE
BUCKEYE
ROVERS
IN THE
GOLD RUSH

An Edition of Two Diaries

Edited by H. Lee Scamehorn, Edwin P. Banks,
and Jamie Lytle-Webb

With an Introduction by H. Lee Scamehorn

Revised and Enlarged Edition

Ohio University Press
Athens

Library of Congress Cataloging-in-Publication Data
The Buckeye Rovers in the Gold Rush : an edition of two diaries /
    edited by H. Lee Scamehorn, Edwin P. Banks, and Jamie Lytle-
    Webb ; with an introduction by H. Lee Scamehorn — Rev.
    and enl. ed.
        p.   cm.
    Diaries written by John Banks and J. Elza Armstrong.
    Previous ed. published as: The Buckeye Rovers in the Gold
Rush. 1965.
    ISBN 0–8214–0922–0. — ISBN 0–8214–0923–9 (pbk.)
    1. California—Description and travel—1848–1869.   2.
California—Gold discoveries.   3. Overland journeys to the
Pacific.   4. West (U.S.)—Description and travel—1848–
1860.   5. Banks, John, fl. 1849–1851—Diaries.   6. Arm-
strong, J. Elza—Diaries.   7. Pioneers—California—Diaries.
I. Scamehorn, H. Lee (Howard Lee), 1926– . II. Banks,
Edwin P.   III. Lytle-Webb, Jamie.   IV. Banks, John, fl.
1849–1851.   V. Armstrong, J. Elza.   VI. Buckeye Rovers
in the Gold Rush.
F865.B92   1989
979.4′04–dc19   89–31054
                                                                  CIP

Ohio University Press books are
printed on acid-free paper ∞

ACKNOWLEDGMENTS

Many people contributed to this volume. Mr. John G. Keller, Jr., of Columbus, Ohio, gave permission to publish the Armstrong diary, which his father had given to The Ohio Historical Society many years ago. Mrs. Wilma Wagenblast and Mr. Edwin P. Banks made available and granted permission to publish the diaries of their grandfather, John Banks.

Numerous people associated with libraries and research facilities gave generously of their time in tracing the events and incidents mentioned by the diarists. The editor is particularly grateful for assistance rendered by Dr. James H. Rodabaugh and Dr. Kenneth W. Duckett of The Ohio Historical Society; Mr. Walter W. Wright of Ohio University; Miss Alice Smith of the Wisconsin State Historical Society; and Miss Lucille Fry of the Western History Collections, University of Colorado. Professor George Lobdell and Mr. Ivan Tribe of Ohio University also provided valuable support for the documentation of the manuscripts.

The Graduate School and History Department of the University of Colorado provided funds for the typing, which was ably performed by Mrs. Jacqueline B. Allen and Mrs. Lloyd Carter. Mr. Taylor Culbert and Mrs. Carol Harvey of Ohio University Press offered guidance, editorial assistance, and unlimited patience.

* * *

At the time *The Buckeye Rovers in the Gold Rush* was published in 1965, the middle segment of John Banks's diary, from February 23 to November 23, 1851, was missing and presumed lost forever. In 1987, however, that portion of the record was found and returned to Banks's heirs. At about the same time, The Ohio University Press, unaware that Banks's diary was complete, decided to reissue the book which had been out of print for nearly twenty years. Fortunately, Banks's grandson and great-granddaughter agreed to join the editor of the original publication in preparing the new material for a revised and enlarged edition of *The Buckeye Rovers in the Gold Rush.*

The new edition contains the once-missing portion of the diary, now chapter eight. The editors have taken advantage of the opportunity to correct errors of commission and omission that had been discovered in the original publication. They have also prepared a new map of the gold region. This, together with an index to the Armstrong-Banks diaries will allow readers to follow more accurately the overland trek of the Buckeye Rovers and their search for gold.

Contents

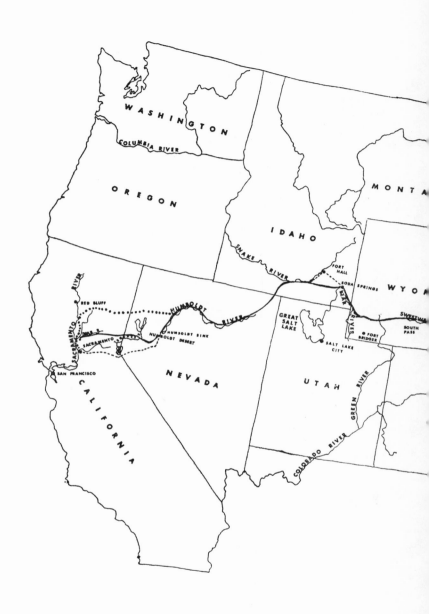

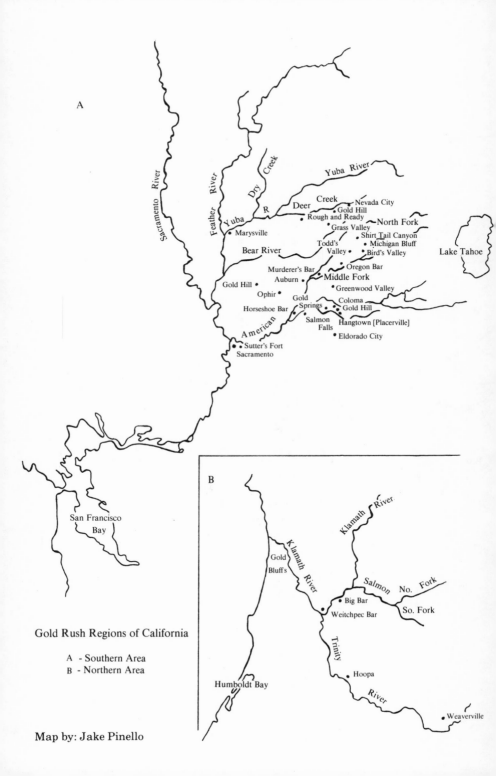

A

Sacramento River

Feather River

Dry Creek

Yuba River

Yuba R

Deer Creek

Nevada City
Gold Hill
Rough and Ready
Grass Valley
Shirt Tail Canyon
Michigan Bluff
Bird's Valley
North Fork

Marysville

Bear River

Todd's Valley

Lake Tahoe

Murderer's Bar
Auburn
Middle Fork
Oregon Bar

Gold Hill
Greenwood Valley

Ophir

Gold Springs
Coloma
Gold Hill

Horseshoe Bar

American

Salmon Falls
Hangtown [Placerville]

Eldorado City

Sutter's Fort
Sacramento

San Francisco Bay

B

Klamath River

Gold Bluffs

Klamath River

Salmon No. Fork

Big Bar
Weitchpec Bar
So. Fork

Trinity

Hoopa

River

Weaverville

Humboldt Bay

Gold Rush Regions of California

A - Southern Area
B - Northern Area

Map by: Jake Pinello

Introduction

The West seemed crowded with gold-seekers, a Columbus newspaper observed in early April, 1849; every stage, steamboat, and road was thronged with Ohioans on their way to the Pacific shore.[1] "Almost every village," the account continued, "furnishes its company, and some two or three." Heavy wagons drawn by oxen and mules rattled through city streets and along country lanes, most of them to river ports—Marietta, Pomeroy, Gallipolis, Portsmouth, and Cincinnati—for passage to St. Joseph and other communities at the head of the trails leading overland to California.

News of gold reaching the Atlantic seaboard the previous summer had set in motion a migration which reached its peak in the following two years. Those who set out for the mining regions that year traveled by sea and combination sea-and-land routes because early autumn storms threatened to close the more direct trails across the West.[2]

When inland navigation reopened the following spring, interior states experienced the excitement restricted until then to the coastal settlements. Fortune hunters, in a headlong rush for *El Dorado*, abandoned jobs and professions, families, and friends. Some traveled to eastern seaports in search of shipping around the Horn, or to Panama, Nicaragua, and Mexico, transfer points on the combination routes to the mines. Most of the emigration swept westward, however, across Texas, down the Old Santa Fe Trail, and assumed the proportions of a stampede along the Oregon-California Trail. Perhaps, as Professor John Walton Caughey has suggested, the historic route of the fur trader up the Platte and over South Pass appealed to a majority of the Forty-Niners because, like the girl next door, it was close at hand.[3]

The momentum of the gold rush surprised and alarmed many observers. One Cincinnati editor estimated that each of Ohio's counties would lose at least 120 persons to the emigration, or about ten thousand in all; a Columbus newspaper placed the state's loss at twice that number.[4] Although both figures were greatly exaggerated, Ohioans, according to the incomplete *U.S. Seventh Census* (1850), formed the third largest American element in California, ranking in order behind New York and Missouri.[5]

When "California fever" raced through southeastern Ohio in the early spring of 1849, a number of residents of Athens County, mostly from Athens, Albany, and Hebbardsville, organized a cooperative venture for traveling overland to the mines. Most of those men—J. Elza Armstrong, John Banks, Asa Condee, Dr. Joseph D. and Hugh Dixon, Denis Drake, Elijah Ferrill, Harvey L. Graham, William Logan, George Reeves, James Shepard, William S. Steadman, and William S. Wilson—stayed together for five months while traveling to California, and maintained close relations for almost three years in the mining region. All but the Dixon brothers, who died there, returned to their homes by the summer of 1852.

Known as the "Buckeye Rovers," the company started from Albany in early April for Pomeroy, where they planned to purchase passage by river steamer to western Missouri. They rested at the close of the first day in Rutland, at which point the "Meigs County Boys" joined forces with the Athens group. The new company was composed of Reuben J. Barnes, James and Joshua Gardner, Charles and John S. Giles, Seth Paine, Dr. J. H. Rathburn, Alonzo Smith, Lorenzo D. Stevens, and Solomon Townshend. The enlarged troupe which continued southward the following day represented a typical cross-section of southern Ohio, being made up of farmers, mechanics, doctors, a lawyer, and a newspaper editor.

The trip from Pomeroy to western Missouri required two weeks, with brief stops at the principal ports on the Ohio and Mississippi rivers. The Ohioans traveled to Cincinnati aboard the packet *Monongahela,* then, after less than one day's delay, continued to St. Louis on the *Pontiac.*[6] The final and longest portion of the trip, to the upper Missouri, required eight days because the *Saluda* experienced mechanical breakdowns soon after leaving the Mississippi. Because of the delay the steamer did not go to St. Joseph as scheduled, but put in at Lexington when the channel fell to less than five feet above Camden.[7] There the Buckeye gold-seekers decided to make their "outfit" for the overland journey.

Lexington, a thriving community on the south bank of the river about seventy miles southeast of St. Joseph, vied with that city, Westport, and Independence for the emigrant trade. It boasted of a fine location in a rich farming region; abundant and cheap horses, mules, and oxen; and "goods of every description" for California-bound travelers.[8] Wagon-makers, tinners, gunsmiths, and other craftsmen catered to the demands of the fortune-hunters who arrived by every steamboat from down river.

The Buckeye Rovers and their companions from Rutland purchased equipment and provisions for a four- or five-month journey across the West. Within three days the Athens group had three wagons, eleven yoke of oxen, one yoke of cows, and requisite stocks of food; they were ready to start for St. Joseph and the trail for the Platte River.

Sometime between May 2 and 9, the time spent in St. Joseph, the Ohioans formed a train for the trip through nearly two thousand miles of uncharted land. The Buckeye Rovers, and perhaps the Meigs County group as well, had previously created a copartnership with a common fund and pledges of mutual assistance to the close of the journey.[9] The two companies, plus Caleb Ferris of Michigan and W. H. Smith of Wisconsin, comprised a traveling unit with Dr. Dixon as captain to enforce general regulations adopted by common consent against the dangers and uncertainties of the trail. Similar organizations were almost universally employed by Forty-Niners.[10]

Rather than wait two or three days for a chance to cross on the ferry at St. Joseph the Ohioans drove north, probably to Savannah Landing (Amazonia); on reaching the opposite bank of the Missouri they returned to the main road which ran almost straight west about ninety miles to the Big Blue River, near the point where the trail came in from Independence. Tormented by heavy rains and unseasonable temperatures which retarded grass for the oxen, they turned northward over rolling plains to the Platte.

They passed Fort Kearny, the first military outpost on the Oregon-California Trail, in the flood tide of emigration. An official count, started there the second week of May, indicated that 500 wagons had passed the post by the 18th; thereafter the average exceeded 300 daily until the 28th, when 460, including six or seven in the Ohio train, rolled by in a single day.[11] Traffic then declined rapidly; within a week most of the trains were on the North Platte, straining to reach the eastern slope of the Rocky Mountains.

Paralleling the Platte to the junction of its two forks, the Buckeye group followed a well-marked road on the South Platte as far as the present site of Brule, Nebraska, before crossing over to the other branch at a point near what is now the community of Lewellen. They followed the North Platte for two weeks, pausing briefly at Fort Laramie, then turned to the Sweetwater River, skirted Independence Rock and Devil's Gate, and reached the summit of the Rockies at South Pass.

The wagon train disintegrated on the Sweetwater. All of the Rutland men, except Solomon Townshend, had for some time complained of Dixon's slow pace designed to conserve the strength of the oxen. Determined to push ahead to gold, they finally left the Buckeye Rovers on July 2. Within a week they had gained by one day's march on their companions from Athens County.

Beyond the Continental Divide the Buckeye Rovers traveled almost straight west to the Big Sandy, taking at that point the road to the right, Sublette's Cutoff, which avoided Fort Bridger and Salt Lake City. They entered the present state of Idaho near what is now Montpelier, turned northward in the direction of Fort Hall on the old trail, but struck west again near Soda Spring onto Hudspeth's, or Emigrant's Cutoff, a new road to Raft River.

All trails—from Soda Spring, Fort Hall, and Salt Lake City —converged on the headwaters of the Humboldt River, in what is now the northeastern portion of Nevada. Banks and Armstrong reached that point in early August. In the following three weeks they paralleled that watercourse to its Sink, a broad marsh where it disappeared into the ground, as if soaked up by the parched terrain. Beyond, a sixty-mile desert crossing separated the emigrants from the Sierra Nevadas, the final barrier before the gold regions. Rejecting the longer,

treacherous Lassen's Cutoff to Feather River and the southern trail to the Carson, they started across the barren waste
for the Truckee. Had the desert trek been ten miles longer,
as Professor David M. Potter has suggested, most of the emigrants would have perished within sight of their goal.[12]

Entering the mining area at Steep Hollow on Bear River,
they paused to prospect there and as far southward as the
North Fork of the American. After failing to find large quantities of gold, all but three of the group, determined to have
a permanent home for the approaching wet season, pushed
on to Sacramento and finally settled in Cold Spring, near
Coloma. Armstrong, Barnes, and Logan went to Deer Creek
before locating for the winter in Vernon, near the junction of
the Sacramento and Feather rivers.[13]

The Ohioans enjoyed varied success over a period of three
years. Some of the men who worked the Yuba or its tributaries acquired enough wealth to return home after a single
season. Those who stayed on the American had little reason
for optimism. Prospecting, though a necessity, was expensive,
involving no income while living costs remained high. Too
frequently, Banks observed, the miner who constantly pur-
sued a rich claim never found it; he learned that while searching the mountains in 1850, others had taken from ground
near his cabin at Cold Spring immense fortunes, and from a
place he had previously dismissed as worthless.

At the start of another wet season in 1850 the Buckeye
miners, all of whom had hoped to return to Ohio that year,
decided to find new claims. Most of the group established
winter homes in Ophir, a small settlement west of Auburn
in the midst of promising dry diggings. There eleven men
who had crossed the plains together held a reunion after one
year in the mines. Few were rich, but all had enjoyed some

success. Each man, according to Banks, had a few hundred dollars.

When Ophir, like the American, proved unprofitable, they explored the main streams. Subsequently they returned to the Ophir-Gold Hill diggings, west of Auburn. Dame Fortune, that capricious nymph, granted their wishes for the lucky strike. The Gardners, Graham, Paine, and two or three others found at Gold Hill placers that yielded rich rewards. Banks and some of his companions, including Armstrong, Barnes, and Ferrill, bought into the Ophir mines in the spring of 1852; within a few weeks they were ready to start home.

At the close of May, 1852, Armstrong, Banks, Barnes, Ferrill, Reeves, and Charles Giles, together with other Ohioans, left the mining regions forever. From San Francisco they sailed to New York, via Panama, aboard the Pacific Mail steamer *Tennessee*. After a trip of only six weeks, a marked contrast to their overland journey, they reached Athens, ending the adventures of the Buckeye Rovers.

The story of the Forty-Niners from Athens County has been preserved in diaries written by Armstrong and Banks. The first, a brief description of events on the overland trail, and the second, a more revealing account of experiences en route to California and in the mines, form an unusually complete history of one company over a period of more than three years.

Many who participated in the gold rush wrote of their experiences; emigrants who went by way of the Platte and South Pass in 1849 kept more than one hundred and thirty extant diaries or journals.[14] Ohioans penned at least fifteen, seven of which have been published; the remainder are in libraries, holdings of private collectors, or the possession of heirs of the writers.[15]

Like many of the diaries from that year, Armstrong's reveals a terse, sober style and surprisingly little information about himself, traveling companions, or adventures on the trail. He, like many gold-seekers who crossed the Missouri with high hopes, soon became absorbed in the monotonous routine of life on the road to California—long tiring marches, the hot, blinding sun, the constant quest for grass and water, and the struggle to push ahead as rapidly as possible. Most of the emigrants who started diaries probably threw them away soon after leaving St. Joseph; Armstrong ignored his for a time, then confined his literary efforts to such essentials as condition of the road, weather, important landmarks, and the length of each day's journey.

His small leather-bound diary, prefaced with sketchy notes tracing the movement of the company from Albany to Lexington, opened with a day-to-day record on May 9, the date of departure from St. Joseph. Three weeks later, when traveling on the Platte west of Fort Kearny, Armstrong stopped writing without an explanation; twenty-six days afterwards the entries resumed, again without reason, and continued until he reached the periphery of the mining regions on Bear River.

Internal evidence indicates that Armstrong wrote only for his own satisfaction, perhaps to create a bare record to serve as a reminder in future years. Although a native of Ohio, a descendant of a pioneer family in Athens County, he had no close attachment to home or family, for whom he might have written, as did Banks. An infant at the time of his father's death, Armstrong was entrusted by his mother to the care of grandparents who resided on a farm near Hebbardsville.[16] The gold rush apparently afforded a restless young man of twenty-two years a welcome opportunity for adventure and wealth, and to escape from aging guardians and the tedious life of a farmer.

John Banks, by contrast, filled three small books with much that he deemed worthy of permanent record. The first began in Lexington, April 24, 1849 and closed in California, February 21, 1851, when he sent it home by a friend. Although some attention was devoted to Lexington and the subsequent overland trip to St. Joseph, the main portion consisted of daily entries from May 9 to September 30, the period of travel to the mining regions. The remainder of that volume was devoted to weekly reports of events in California.

For a time, only one of the other two diaries was extant. The record for the second period, from February 23 to November 23, 1851, was sent home by a returning friend, but there is no evidence that it reached its destination. It was missing until the summer of 1987, when a bookdealer determined that a diary in his possession was the missing segment. The third unit of the diary, for the period from November 31, 1851 to June 8, 1852, Banks carried to Ohio. The final entry was written aboard ship in the latitude of Acapulco, bound for Panama. The final segment described the writer's most successful mining operations. Unfortunately, the diary was not protected by a waterproof covering; the script on the first four pages (November 31 to January 11) has deteriorated badly in the past century, making it impossible to transcribe all of the material accurately.

Irish-born, an American by residence for all but two of his thirty years, John Banks was a hard-working, God-fearing farmer who lived with his parents, five sisters, and three brothers near Albany when news of California gold strikes reached southern Ohio. Finding the opportunity for adventure and wealth irresistible, he joined friends and neighbors in the first overland rush.

The Banks family had a tradition of seeking advancement in new lands. Almost two centuries earlier another John Banks—the first of eight so named—had participated in the Irish settlement sponsored by Oliver Cromwell's government. When denied agricultural lands by the cupidity of a trusted friend, he took up the shoemaker's trade in Beggar's Bridge, County Meath (now Rochfortbridge, County Westmeath). Six generations adhered steadfastly to that craft and to the Protestant faith in an impoverished, predominantly Catholic land until 1821, when William and Mary Ann Scott Banks, hoping to escape religious strife and to provide a better life for their children, migrated to America.[17]

William Banks, aided in time by son John, became the proprietor of a shoemaker's shop on New York's Hudson Street. The family remained there for thirteen years, during which time it grew from four to nine members with the addition of three girls and two boys.[18] One more son was born in 1833, one year following another move, that time to the farm near Albany. Reasons of health prompted a change of climate; William and four of his children suffered from the debilitating effects of consumption.

When "gold fever" raced through southern Ohio in the early months of 1849, John Banks eagerly joined other residents of the region around Albany in planning an overland expedition to California. At the moment of decision, however, he was torn between devotion to family and the prospect of wealth at the journey's end. For days, perhaps weeks, he brooded, not knowing what to do. Finally, he joined the Buckeye Rovers shortly before their departure.

Separated from parents, sisters, and brothers for the first time, Banks sought through the pages of his diaries a close attachment with loved ones and familiar surroundings, though removed by time and distance. For this reason, his record of the trail and the mining regions is more personal than is usual for the diaries written in 1849. His reveals, above all, one man's varying moods: the impact of frustrations and joys of daily existence in a new and ever-changing environment.

Whether along the Platte, or on the American, his thoughts never strayed far from family, home, and faith. Scenes and events were depicted so as to be meaningful to those who remained in Ohio, who, in fact, shared every mile of the trek to California and each day's pursuit of gold in remote diggings. The diaries are to be valued because, unlike many others written at that time, they were not for a wide audience, but for an intimate family circle.

Forceful and often witty, Banks's record reveals the hardships, dangers, and triumphs of a small band in an inhospitable environment. He mentions problems which absorbed all diarists: scarcity of grass; the persistence of alkali, a threat to man and beast; hostile Indians in Nevada and California; and internal dissension within his own and other trains. He also deviates from traditional topics, emphasizing scenes and curiosities which escaped most writers.

California, as depicted by Banks, was a scene of blustering activity, the land of quick fortunes for some and lingering hopelessness for others. Men were traveling in all directions seeking rich placers. Claims were worked and reworked, as every ravine was torn up; within a year dirt was washed for the fourth or fifth time. Alternating between hope and despair, miners persisted in their search. Some, as did most of the Buckeye Rovers, acquired modest fortunes; but for every success there were many failures.

The pursuit of wealth required the application of a crude mining technology. Banks employed the standard tools— pick and shovel—to reach the gold which he separated, in turn, by several methods: first the pan, simplest of all mining implements, and in time the cradle, long tom, and sluice. His descriptions of mining practices throw little light on what has long been known, but his narrative presents some interesting insights into one man's attempt to find more efficient ways of extracting gold from the soil.

Traditionally, gold has served as a magnet to draw men of varied backgrounds and persuasions to remote lands. California, site of the first large gold rush in American experience, attracted, as Banks observed, its share of undesirables. The principal evils in the mining camps were murder, stealing, gambling, intemperance, cursing, and violation of the Sabbath. Too often men who doubted their own manhood or courage assumed that the taking of another life was a mark of knighthood. Others seemed determined to make money by any means; during the first spring exodus to high mountain streams, mule thieves outnumbered mules. And when abandoned women completed the awful state of society, gambling was finally mated!

Deep religious convictions which prompted hasty criticism of others produced, however, a keen awareness of scenes which too often escaped gold-seeking journalists. Nature's beauty, the magnificence of God's handiwork, was truly astonishing: stately landmarks, refreshing springs, grand forests, and the majestic Rockies or Sierra Nevadas were among the wonders of the world. The rugged terrain of the American River, although to the miner nothing but an obstacle in the way of gold, would someday serve as subjects for artists who delight the world with breath-taking grandeur.

Banks's main interests, judging from the diaries, were, in addition to theology, history, philosophy, botany, zoology, and geology. His grasp of physical detail was indeed marvelous, and he could tell a story forcefully and completely in a few words. Surprisingly little escaped his notice. At the close of the day, or later during the quiet of the Sabbath, his reflections on events and scenes worthy of record for posterity frequently dwelled on flora and fauna, the geography and topography of his immediate locale, and varied aspects of human relations in a strange land.

The diaries of Armstrong and Banks differ sharply in style and content. Brief, even laconic, Armstrong seldom says anything that his companion does not state at greater length and with more meaning, yet the very contrast brings into focus divergent personalities whom the gold rush affected in varying ways. When the two records are read together, Banks emerges as one of those unusual men, not uncommon in the pioneering experience of America, who combined determination of purpose with faith, balanced by sympathetic understanding of human failings.

The two diaries present similar problems in their preparation for publication. Erratic spelling and punctuation have been standardized, and, for the sake of clarity, unbroken phrases and clauses have been separated into logical sentences.

Great care has been taken to preserve, in so far as possible, the original flavor of the diaries, even to the extent of compromising with modern standards for proper English usage. Some improper verb tenses, peculiarities in spelling, and unrelated thoughts within a single sentence have been retained simply because their alteration would have distorted the context of the record. In an effort to enhance readability all abbreviations have been written out, and numbers have been changed into word values.

Occasionally words have been supplied if the omission was obviously an oversight, or the consequence of the arduous conditions under which the diaries were written. Where the writing had faded beyond recognition, or edges of the pages had crumbled with age, logical word sequences have been provided within brackets to indicate that the original could not be accurately transcribed.

BANKS FAMILY PORTRAIT, C.1876
Left to right: John Edwin, John, James Alfred (in his mother's arms), William Addison, Cynthia Adelia, Sarah Maria, and Clara Judson.

The Buckeye Rovers in the GOLD RUSH

Lexington to Fort Kearny
April 24—May 28

[The diarists and their companions from Athens and Meigs counties traveled from Pomeroy, Ohio to Lexington, Missouri by river steamer. Unable to reach their original destination, St. Joseph, they debarked at Lexington to purchase livestock, equipment, and provisions for the overland trail. Banks began his daily record in that city; Armstrong started his account two and a half weeks later on leaving St. Joseph for California.]

APRIL 24: [*Banks*] This day we reached Lexington which is situated on the Missouri River.[1] It is a very flourishing town and a remarkable illustration of the rapid growth of the West. Nine or ten years since its site was a wilderness. Its population at present is nine thousand. The houses are mostly brick. Its court house is a noble building showing much public spirit, but there is disease gnawing at its vitals. Slavery has a strong hold on this place considering its recent settlement. The surrounding country is very rich. I saw that hemp is a great staple. This region has many natural advantages. I found the people not wholly insensible to the evil of slavery; they are aware of its being a drawback to their prosperity. We made our outfit at this place and will be ready to leave it on the 28th.

APRIL 28: [*Banks*] We had much trouble crossing the river in a flat boat and were delayed a considerable time yoking the oxen. This day we made five miles and encamped in a grove on the edge of a beautiful prairie. We had good water; the grass good for the season which is late.

APRIL 29: [*Banks*] How strange the sound it is Sunday, but it passes as any other day, except that this day my mind dwells on home and those hopes founded on the resurrection of Christ from the dead. This day we traveled [word missing] miles.

APRIL 30: [*Banks*] This day a most beautiful country opened to our view. I had read of prairies; I had seen a prairie, but this sight was unexpected. Rich hills skirted by lovely valleys of almost inexhaustable fertility intersperced by groves of timber in many places laid off in large farms is indeed grand. The grass not very good. We feed corn, price twenty-five cents per bushel. The health of the company pretty good; mine excellent. Distance traveled this day thirteen miles. Weather clear and cold.

MAY 1: [*Banks*] The face of the country much the same. The springs are very refreshing after journeying in the dust. I now begin to feel what walking is; sore feet and tired legs— poor companions for a long journey.

MAY 2: [*Banks*] We arrived at St. Joseph, a dirty town on the frontier of Missouri. Its growth has been very rapid, but its appearance is uninviting. Here we begin to see what an excitement California has created. On the river then [Lexington] was confusion enough; here it is a complete jam. Two ferrys are so busy there is no chance for us except we wait two or three days. There is a new ferry four miles up the river; here we intend to cross to the home of the red man.[2] Here we met Dr. Dixon and his brother Hugh, who left St. Louis three days later than we did.

MAY 9: [Armstrong] *Left St. Joseph for the upper ferry.*

[*Banks*] Left St. Joseph for the upper ferry; hard driving through a deep forest. At the ferry I saw a colored man going to the land of gold prompted by the hope of redeeming a wife and seven children. Success to him. His name is James Taylor.

MAY 10: [Armstrong] *Crossed the river and drove to the bluffs and camped.*

[*Banks*] Crossed the river rowing a flat boat against the stream; not easy work. We encamped four miles from the river on the edge of a prairie.

MAY 11: [Armstrong] *Started for the main road. Had some difficulty in reaching the road. Distance eleven miles.*

[*Banks*] We had some difficulty in reaching the road. Our distance ten miles.

MAY 12: [Armstrong] *Crossed Wolf and Bear creeks. Distance fifteen.*

[*Banks*] The sky is cloudy. We crossed two streams, Wolf and Bear creeks. This evening we had dozens of Indians constantly near us. Some of the younger ones shooting with bows and arrows for money, the others gazing intently at the pale faces. They are quite civil and bear a good name, but are wretchedly lazy. Their huts are miserable hovels. Distance fifteen miles.

MAY 13: [Armstrong] *Sunday. We started for the missionary station.*[3]

[*Banks*] We started for the missionary station. I heard a sermon from a good speaker and was much pleased to hear the Indian children sing. It was a scene I shall always remember with pleasure. I was much struck by the appearance of a boy of powerful muscle about seven years old whose contenance has a strange mixture of fierceness and good humor. Poor fellow, I would like to know what the future has in store for him! This day Mr. Paine lost a pony costing thirty-five dollars. It had been stolen from an old Indian of good character. The proof was clear. Distance three miles.

MAY 14: [Armstrong] *A raining; continued until ten o'clock. We started on our journey. The land lays well and a little rolling. Distance eleven miles.*

[*Banks*] This morning I was on watch. About daybreak I saw a wolf some five rods from camp. This morning very wet and stormy, which delayed us until nine o'clock, six being our usual time. We put out our cattle about four a.m., and generally encamp four p.m. Much talk of cholera and smallpox.[4] Grass good. The general face of the country pleasing. Distance eleven miles.

MAY 15: [Armstrong] *Traveled twenty-five miles. The land lays about the same as before mentioned.*

[*Banks*] Weather fine and roads good. "Go ahead" is our motto today. At a turn in the road we saw shirts, vests, and other apparel strewed near a new-made grave. A few lines on a stick read: "Here we buried Mr. Adams, then passed on." This day we passed fifty wagons. Distance twenty-five miles.

MAY 16: [Armstrong] *Jenkins came up with us. We crossed the Nemaha Creek. The distance twenty.*

[*Banks*] General Jenkins of Wisconsin and family joined us, four men, one woman, four children.[5] Our number of wagons now eight. The report today is the Pawnees are coming down on us. Sickness is very prevalent. I am led to the opinion that intemperance is the main cause of our health. Mine good. Distance twenty.

MAY 17: [Armstrong] *The sky is covered with dark clouds. Passed a grave where there were three men buried in one grave; died of cholera. Distance fifteen miles.*

[*Banks*] Cloudy with an appearance of rain. "Much sickness in your camp?" is now a common question. Deaths numerous. Passed a grave containing three persons, all of Illinois. Distance fifteen miles.

MAY 18: [Armstrong] *We started from our encampment at six o'clock today. We passed one hundred teams and with the rest a small government train bound for Fort Childs.*[6] *They buried one of the soldiers today. Distance twenty-two miles.*

[*Banks*] All in good spirits. The road is dotted by wagons fore and aft as far as the eye can reach, which is no short distance. The face of the country is undulating, one vast prairie having no timber except on the watercourses; scarcely any stone; and very poor water. This day we passed one hundred wagons, among which was a government train destined for Fort Charles [Childs]. They are a dissipated set; at noon they buried one of the men, death by intemperance. He received military honors. The ceremony is imposing. This is the burial I was present at. It is simply this: he was sewed in his blanket, then committed to the earth without box or coffin, his grave being not more than two and a half feet deep. The cold sod placed on his bosom, he sleeps in the wilderness. Distance twenty-two.

MAY 19: [Armstrong] *We came to the Big Blue River. We crossed without much difficulty. There were a great many wagons awaiting to cross. There was a grave on the bank of the river. It was a Catholic. The Independence road and St. Joseph road come together.*[7] *Distance fifteen miles.*

[*Banks*] Early this day we crossed the Big Blue.

Two big trains immediately behind us. The water is nearly three feet deep, the stream wide. Such whooping and yelling, "Who Whoy" is amusing. Today we passed the intersection of the Independence road. Saw two graves. The crosses: "I.H. Snow, here lies a Catholic," and "John Graham, died March 21, 1847." The only old graves I have seen. They rest from their journey. Distance fifteen.

MAY 20: [Armstrong] A raining this morning. We passed one grave today. Distance sixteen miles.

[Banks] Rain and very heavy winds constantly blowing. At noon sun showers, rain in very large drops. We saw one grave today. The sickness decreasing. Distance sixteen.

MAY 21: [Armstrong] We passed two large trains today. Seen two buffalo for the first we have seen. They were on the Little Platte. Distance twenty-five.

[Banks] This morning rumor says twenty-two men killed, sixteen wagons burned by Indians a few miles ahead. General Jenkins saw where Indians encamped last night. Each man is preparing himself for action. Passed two trains. Encamped where we had to carry wood and water one mile from the Little Platte. Distance twenty.

MAY 22: [Armstrong] Cold and windy. We passed a company from Columbus, Ohio.[8] They had lost seventy-two head of their cattle. They had them in a corral and they got scared and broke out, they dividing off and were in perfect confusion. This was on the bank of the Blue River. Distance fifteen miles.

[Banks] Cattle out at three a.m. Started before six, crossed the beds of two streams now nearly dry. Those that rise in the prairie soon dry. We are now encamped on a high bluff on the banks of the Little Blue. On this spot a few days since a man accidently shot himself; his grave is near. Half a mile east of us is an encampment from Columbus, Ohio, who lost seventy-two head of cattle. There are white pirates stealing on the road. This company is broken up; here lies the foundation of an Indian tragedy. Distance fifteen miles.

MAY 23: [Armstrong] *Started early this morning up the valley of the Blue. We are in the heart of the Pawnee Indians but none have been seen.*[9] *Distance twenty-two miles.*

[*Banks*] Very cold and cloudy, a fine day for traveling. Roads excellent. We are evidently in the buffalo country; numerous skulls attest to this. Elk horns have been common some days. The frequency with which we see scraps of paper or a small board left telling who is ahead is amusing. One: "The Infantry Company F passed here; all well and in good spirits; plenty of game and good whiskey." They subsequently offered one dollar for a pint of brandy. Some of our men out hunting report much game: elk, antelope, and turkeys. One out yet, J. S. Giles. He was last seen about ten miles off in hot chase of game. We are in the midst of the Pawnee Nation. They are savage and treacherous. We are encamped on Little Blue, a fine stream of swift-running water. Distance twenty miles.

MAY 24: [Armstrong] *It is cold and windy. Remained at our encampment till twelve o'clock and then we started. It commenced raining shortly after we started. We put up early. Distance five miles.*

[*Banks*] Cold and rainy, thunder and lightning with heavy showers all day. Giles came in this morning. He had lodged at a camp four miles east, some of whom saw a man that the Indians had murdered lying on his face, stript of all save his pants and shirt. He had wandered two miles from the road.

We have seen no Indians since we left the mission. They may dread the cholera, as some say; others believe villainy the cause. The multitude that is going is wonderful. It seems as if the whole world was going to market. The face of the country rather broken, the soil gravelly, no timber except on the streams. Health good. Encamped on the Blue in a handsome situation, neighbors near every night. Grass good, cattle in pretty good order. Distance three miles.

MAY 25: [Armstrong] *Cold rain. Roads very muddy. We are encamped on the Blue where we leave it. Distance fourteen miles.*

[*Banks*] On watch at one a.m. Very cold and high winds. Saw much prickly pears. This whole region abounds in a species of rusk; it grows tall, consisting of many joints said to be good for cattle. My lips are very sore, a general complaint. This has been the most boisterous day I have ever seen, the wind is raving. Distance twelve.

MAY 26: [Armstrong] *This morning we prepared ourselves for a hard day's journey but we found no difficulty. Distance ten miles.*

[*Banks*] Left camp at half past six a.m. Morning very cold. Heard that the pilot of the U.S. Infantry was shot by Indians; not dead. Also, the Indians drove in two hunters of a Virginia train. One of Mr. Jenkins' wagons broke an axel about nine o'clock; we waited six hours, then went on. While I was herding our cattle, meditating on the solitude of the place (scarcely anything to relieve the sight), my attention was drawn to large flocks of birds which are exceedingly sociable, getting very near each other; no quarreling, but a sweet voice of recognition. I think they are the buffalo's friend as they kept very near our cattle. Beautiful warblers of the prairie, they are rather less than the robin, in black with red breasts. Mr. Jenkins came up at nine p.m. The weather quite moderate. All well. Some dissatisfaction at being delayed. Distance twelve miles.

MAY 27: [Armstrong] *The weather is warm. When we came in sight of the bluffs of the Platte we seen plenty of buffalo and antelope. We had to swim to an island to get wood. Distance twenty-two miles.*

[*Banks*] This day was beautiful. How often I think of home, of my parting with father and mother, brothers and sisters, all that constitutes home, with many near and dear friends. May I remember them and their precepts. As we neared the Platte River today the number of antelope was astonishing. They are beautiful and very swift. We overtook a company of soldiers on their way to Oregon. All they seem to want is whiskey. The bluffs of the Platte are the prettiest I have ever seen. They are low and conical, resembling madcaps. Yesterday we saw five wagons laden with furs going to the states.[10] Today we passed the Fort Kearny road. Several of the boys crossed the river to get wood. A hard day's travel. Distance twenty miles. All well.

MAY 28: [Armstrong] *Left our encampment, came to Fort Kearny. There was a great many people there. The houses were built with sod. The fort is situated about half a mile from the river and, as I should consider, very poorly fortified.*[11] *Last week there were two thousand Sioux came down on the Pawnees and whipped them, and took some of them prisoners. Distance nineteen miles.*

[*Banks*] Left camp half past seven. Road bad. The

valley of the Platte is low and in places marshy, though the soil and subsoil is sandy. It never will be arable land. We passed Fort Kearny this day; it is the first western fort I have seen. It is on low land some half mile from the river. It consists of about twenty houses made of sod, some roofed with the same material, walls two feet thick. They must be very warm. There is neither blockhouse nor palisade. A few soldiers and two or three cannon are all the evidence one has that it is not some outlandish village. Some of our men wrote home from this fort. It has a store and a blacksmith shop. Last week two thousand Sioux came down on the Pawnees at this place. They found a man and boy with some emigrants. They killed the man and were carrying off the boy when the dragoons came on them and released the boy. I saw him. One would think that men who left home together would in this wilderness feel outside pressure sufficient to bind them together, but such is not the case. Today I hear two companies have broken up and, indeed, we have not always the best spirit among ourselves. This evening we had to resort to buffalo chips which are here plenty. In some places this plain is white with the buffalo's bones. We thought we saw a herd yesterday. We are encamped half a mile from the river. Distance twenty miles.

Fort Kearny to South Pass

May 29—July 5

[The Ohioans crossed the rolling plains west of the Missouri to the Big Blue River, then turned northward to strike the Platte one day's journey east of Fort Kearny, the first of three new outposts on the Oregon-California Trail. Moving westward in the floodtide of emigration, they passed the fort during their twentieth day on the road. They spent exactly one month along the Platte, or its forks, before crossing to the Sweetwater and South Pass.]

MAY 29: [Armstrong] *We traveled on the flats of the Platte; nothing but the bluffs. They are five or six miles wide. Distance fifteen miles.*

[Banks] Left camp early. A hard day's drive. Roads bad. The swells hard to pass. Distance twenty-two miles.

MAY 30: [Armstrong] *Raining, raining very hard. Jenkins left us today. Distance twelve miles.*

[Banks] It rained very hard in the night. Commenced at two and rained until daylight. Grass poor. Left camp half past eight, came to good grass half past eleven, stopped to feed. Saw a man going back; the journey is not what many expected it to be. We have had no worse times than we expected. Our route for several days is along the Platte which is here wide and noble. We are now above Grand Island. Plenty of snakes, green spotted and rattle. Six of the latter kind killed in less than half an acre. Winds high today. I often see proof that all plans of reform which do enlighten and ennoble are futile pledges, are at best fences easily climbed over. This afternoon I was in a prairie dog village. I saw many of these strange little creatures. This village covers some two hundred acres. They are quite common in this region. We have seen many oxen and mules dead. Distance ten miles.

MAY 31: [Armstrong] *Cold and wet.*

[*Banks*] Cold and wet. Left usual time, traveled until nine. Left camp at one p.m., went on through rain. Last evening General Jenkins left us because we traveled faster than he wished. They were a hindrance to us. The roads bad this day principally owing to late rains. Lips very sore, caused by cold heavy winds. Distance ten miles.

JUNE 1: [*Banks*] Brother William's birthday; twenty-four years since I had a brother. That day is fresh in my memory. This, like that, is a fine day. Six wagons laden with furs from Fort Laramie passed today. Went eight miles back from the road to hunt the form in which sand is molded by weather. It is grand beyond description. Much signs of game. Saw but four antelope. Roads better. Saw an Irish woman bringing hens to California; says they are game. This afternoon saw a young antelope in a man's arms; very handsome. Some clouds. Distance seventeen miles.

JUNE 2: [*Banks*] Left camp half past six. Day fine. Several of our men out hunting; game plenty but greenhorns can't catch them. Heard wolves barking, saw two running. Wagons generally too much laden; many throwing away pork, some wishing to sell other items.[1] Saw a woman going some two or three miles after a little black dog which had been chased by many supposing it some wild animal. Her father in hot pursuit after her vowing he would kill the dog if he found it with her. Along the Platte you see paths at but short intervals which are made by the buffaloes coming from the bluffs to water. Yesterday three men went eighteen miles back to hunt. Saw vast quantities of game and were bringing in some when they found that they themselves were chased. They had a hard race for eight miles. There were eleven well-armed Indians yelling savagely. Camped on the Platte. Distance eighteen miles.

JUNE 3: [*Banks*] Left camp half past seven. Went more than a mile for water; very poor, which is generally the case since we crossed the Missouri. The face of the country is somewhat changed. Puddling stone shows itself. In some places the earth is encrusted with salt; much of the water taken from wells (which you may have by digging a few feet) is saltish. Saw the soap plant, a little like a pineapple, leaves sharply pointed. Saw a very large wolf dead on the road. Eight or nine buffaloes killed near this place. We have some meat for supper. The emigrants seem friendly and liberal. Weather very fine. Roads good, grass middling, wood scarce. Encamped on the Platte. Distance sixteen miles.

JUNE 4: [*Banks*] Remained in camp to change our wagons, being persuaded the projections a hindrance and stiff tongues a folly for this journey. Several men went to hunt on an island in the Platte. Saw a herd of buffaloes but killed none. Mr. Steadman's gun burst, breaking lock, stock, and barrel. Happily no one hurt. In the afternoon a serious altercation between our captain and some of our men about the division of labor. Worked hard. At the junction of South Fork. All well. Six hundred wagons passed today.

JUNE 5: [*Banks*] Left half past six. Road close to the bluffs, seven or eight miles from the river. Forded the river. It is over a mile wide in an ordinary stage, yet but little more than two feet deep. Walked through. Saw Indians of the Sioux Nation; smoked the pipe of peace. A man bringing groceries to sell asks one dollar a pint for brandy; others rather lower. Would advise those coming this route to bring court plaster for lips, nose, and perhaps ears; mine sore. Slept on the ground last night. The wind so violent I can scarcely write lying on the ground under the wagon to shelter the paper. Some Indians in camp now. Distance fourteen miles.

JUNE 6: [*Banks*] Last night very wet. Got wet in bed. Rainy in the forenoon, cloudy in the afternoon. Passed through the Indian encampment; two hundred wigwams, one thousand men, women, and children, many of them fine looking. Some villainous white gave some of them liquor for a robe. Saw one drunk. Clothing of skins and blankets, some are almost naked. Not very honest. Tried to steal a horse of a man. All seemed friendly. Their huts made of hides of buffalo attached to long poles conical in structure. Armed with guns, hatchets, bows and arrows tipped with iron, their objective the extermination of the Pawnees. Today the breeze was fragrant with the scent of southernwood. The sundial a very common plant here; many others of which I have no knowledge. Crossed a ridge from the South to the North Fork. Saw some buffaloes at a distance. Encamped on the last fork. Half a dozen camps near us. Cattle like large droves going east. Plenty of water, no wood, not even a bust. Distance twenty miles.

JUNE 7: [*Banks*] Last night some rain and wind. On watch at one a.m. Heard wolves howling dismally at daylight. Left before six. Passed over a ridge. Nooned in sight of the river.

The face of the country changed; very sandy soil, thin, scarcely any water. This evening rainy with high winds. Rather cold. Feet very sore. Had a long walk. Distance twenty-two miles.

JUNE 8: [*Banks*] Left camp at six. Fine day. As I was walking on I saw a Mr. Gilmore emigrating to Oregon who accidently shot himself through the calf of the leg while putting a cap on his pistol.[2] He was in great pain. Five who left home with hearts beating warm with hope now rest in their lone cold graves; friends may weep but their trouble is over. Fire-arms carelessly handled are often death's messengers. This afternoon the road was bad but we were compensated by finding many springs of pure water. One place we called Cedar Springs; I shall never forget it. Four miles farther, after passing over a remarkably rough ridge, we drove down Ash Hollow.[3] Here are some noble springs. Large trees and wild roses make a pleasing contrast with the surrounding country. Pleasure is often mixed with pain; one of our wagons upset. Fortunately, the damage was not great. We were not delayed more than thirty minutes. We are encamped near an Indian village. We are yet on the Platte. Almost eaten up by mosquitoes. The evening cloudy. Distance eighteen miles.

JUNE 9: [*Banks*] Rained in the night; drizzling until eight a.m., when we left camp. Deep sand and a rough road all the distance. The scenery grand. Lofty, rocky bluffs almost like masonry constantly greet the eye. Saw one man returning; says he can't go all the way. Has money enough; loves his wife more than gold. George Reeves sick, has the dysentery. Saw a man who had a horse stolen, the first case of the kind. The grass this year is better than usual. Bryant says this was a sandy plain when he passed.[4] There is more or less grass all over—mostly poor next the bluffs. Where we are encamped it is good. The quantity of skeletons of buffaloes needs eyesight to convey an adequate idea; everywhere you see them. The vast number of emigrants has driven the buffaloes from the road. We see but few and those at a great distance. Flowers of many varieties and great beauty are daily seen. A white flower somewhat like the wild rose whitens the plains in many places. Evening dark and windy. This is considered a wet season. Our cattle tired. Distance sixteen miles.

JUNE 10: [*Banks*] Last night the lightning was as vivid as I have ever seen. The rain fell in torrents. The man on guard saw a person outside the camp; he called twice, the third he was standing waiting for the next flash of lightning to fire when he found him one of our own men. Men can never be too cautious where life is concerned. We saw two trees this day in which dead Indians were placed by their friends. They are rolled in skins and placed on a platform (formed by sticks from limb to limb), a tin cup, moccasins, and other articles left with them. The nightly storm sings their requiem. Saw Mormons returning to the states from Salt Lake. They gave good encouragement as to grass. The names and mottoes on wagons in some measure indicate the characters of the owners: the "Red Rover," the "Pirate," the "Ass," the "Passia Bird." [5] Some Missourians full of zeal five years old have "Polk and Dallas." The chained lightning this evening presented a most grand and sublime spectacle. We are not far from the spot where the Chimney Rock is first discerned in the distance. We are on the lookout. Distance sixteen miles.

JUNE 11: [*Banks*] Last night the wettest yet. Thunder and lightning, rain in torrents. This morning, after a hard night and much loss of rest, I was awakened by mosquitoes. To say they were in the thousands would convey no adequate idea of their vast numbers; they were in swarms, every place biting like wolves. The sky is clear and looks as if last night's storm was a dream. Crossed streams not more than three inches deep that were four or five feet in the night. Saw a wagon whose owners were in a bad fix, having lost their team. The roads bad, sometimes deep sand or swampy. Saw Chimney Rock and Court House first this afternoon.[6] They are both in view this moment. They are certainly grand and pleasing objects to the traveler on these plains. For several days we see wagons on the opposite side of the river coming from Council Bluffs. This evening cloudy as usual. Distance twenty miles.

JUNE 12: [*Banks*] Rain, rain, rain last night—rain today. Two of our men went to the Court House. I was too tired to go. At noon I started for Chimney Rock which I ascended. The prospect is vast and grand, the rock itself wonderful, standing apart from the bluffs with its tall spire reaching toward the sky. It is some three hundred or four hundred feet in height. I went up its side and recorded my name; among them I saw that of Thomas Pierce of Zanesville. Fifteen miles from this rock to Scott's Bluff is one series of wonders. The soul must be cold that can calmly view these scenes. The powers of water and of wind here revel in all their glory. A palace, a strong fortification with its lofty walls, the wrecks of former greatness, seem ranged along the plain. I have seen two pyramids this day, complete, actual pyramids in shape; nature's work, not man's, some two hundred or three hundred feet high. Imagine yourself in the center of a semicircle; before you stand tall peaks from whose tops you see the Rocky Mountains one hundred miles distant. On your right a lofty wall assuming wonderous forms, some level on the top with a rock like some giant's sentry box. On the left the bluffs are torn by the rushing flood, dark, narrow, lofty, and sublime. Distance twenty miles.

JUNE 14: [7] [*Banks*] On the morning watch. Very cold. As we were ascending Scott's Bluffs we saw a funeral.[8] A Mr. Dunn of Illinois died of cholera after ten hours' illness. His friends say he leaves a wife and child to mourn their loss. Aged twenty-five. From the bluffs I saw the Rocky Mountains towering toward the sky. Laramie's peak stands frowning on the plain in lofty pride among his fellows. The wanderer from the Atlantic stands amazed to think he is in the presence of that lofty chain which stretches through this continent. This day fine, evening cloudy, roads good except one a dangerous slide. Grass poor. Large sand hills barren blown in fantastic forms by the wind. Distance twenty miles.

JUNE 15: [*Banks*] Some rain last night. This day fine. Now raining. Saw a large government train, light dragoons and stores, destined for Fort Laramie.[9] Much sickness on the road. George Reeves very sick yet. Feel very much tired and almost sick. The roads in the afternoon deep sand. Wood plenty, water good. Encamped on a branch of the Platte. Distance twenty-two.

JUNE 16: [*Banks*] Left camp half past six. Roads good. Crossed Laramie's Fork of the Platte at Fort Laramie. The ford is deep, current very swift, and hard to stem. Crossed safely. Saw the fort. Its appearance is military and neat. Did not go in. Wrote home from this place. Traveled six miles further. Roads sandy, grass poor, wood plenty.

The waste of provisions and property on this road is truly wonderful. Some three thousand pounds of iron in one place.

Wagons worth seventy-five to one hundred dollars broken up, chains and harnass, saddles, and large quantities of tolerable good clothing. Piles of bacon and in one place some three hundred pounds of good flour, pilot bread in large quantities. Anything that impedes our progress, not necessary to life, is cast away as worthless. Many are changing their mode of travel from wagons to pack saddles. Costly trunks torn to pieces. Wagon tires and every kind of irons literally strewed along the road. Gold ahead! Men seem reckless to all save that. Encamped on Laramie's Fork. Poor grass. Distance eighteen miles.

JUNE 17: [Banks] Intended to remain in camp this day; grass too poor. Started early. Roads deep sand. Weather exceedingly warm. Saw a human skull supposed an Indian's. Hard for man and cattle; dust in clouds. We are now in the Black Hills, which are not very high. I think they are so-named from a small growth of pine and cedar which give them at a distance a black appearance. At noon we camped at the most wonderful spring I have ever seen. The water is slightly warm in quantity like a millrace; quality sweet and clear as crystal. It is named Warm Spring.

This is an appropriate time to notice other of nature's works. The little ant is everywhere busy. The prairie is covered with small hillocks, some three feet in diameter, often eighteen inches high. Where the soil is loamy it is soon covered with grass. In a gravelly soil they make their excavations by carrying out grains of gravel as large as rice, some larger, completely covering the top. The laborer is not more than one half an inch long. Today I saw several horns of mountain sheep; they are larger than three or four buffalo's horns. One measured nearly eighteen inches long and sixteen in circumference, and weighed not less than ten pounds. The nature of the country is changed. Today we drank of some springs of pure water. The water in the streams is clear and sweet. Land broken and grass poor. More timber than we have seen for many hundred miles, much of it is pine of middling size. Distance twelve miles.

JUNE 18: [*Banks*] Left camp half past five. Roads firm but rather rough. This day very warm, dust troublesome. Saw some Ashtabula men who say that Joshua R. Giddings is regarded as a patriarch among his neighbors.[10] This day threw away what cost us ten or fifteen dollars: chains, beans, salt, and lead. Encamped on Bitterwater Creek—a misnomer, it is sweet. Good grass here on the bottoms. Distance fifteen miles.

JUNE 19: [*Banks*] Left camp six. Roads very rough and sandy. Wild sage is very large here and grows in great abundance. Here we see better timber than on any upland since we left the Missouri. A few miles this side of that river you leave all timber except on the watercourses, or some place where the fire cannot reach it. In deep ravines which are dry at this season you see cedar; near water, cottonwood; on the hills, pine, often two feet in diameter. Fire has not power to destroy on account of the shortness of the grass. Though grass is short, flowers are numerous and beautiful. We passed Laramie's peak this day. On the north side it is covered with snow for a considerable distance down. No other peak is high enough to have any. It is very rugged. During the past week we have seen several dead oxen and some so lame as to be left. This journey is exceedingly hard on cattle. Encamped about one half mile from a small stream on a hill. Grass tolerably good. Distance sixteen miles.

JUNE 20: [*Banks*] Left camp early. Roads very hilly, more so than I had ever seen. The Rocky Mountains in full view. Yesterday some emigrants killed two buffaloes near us. We have a large supply of fresh meat. Do not like it as well as the flesh of our domestic animals. In every case those that have been killed by emigrants, as far as I have heard, were males. We heard that eight men were killed by drinking from a spring three miles east of Chimney Rock, some distance from the road. We did not see it. The water, it is said, is pleasant to the taste. We nooned at the La Bonte, a rapid, clear stream fresh from the mountains. Grass poor. This afternoon traveled in a volcanic region; everything bears the marks of fire. The earth is like burned bricks, the stone either black or calcined. In one place there is no vegetation; the surface is covered with pumice stone. One feels a sense of awe in viewing such scenes. We are encamped in the midst of it. As I sit in camp I raise my eyes; in every direction the ridges are burned and bare; a little thin grass on the sides is all that relieves the sight. The day clear and cold. Distance eighteen.

JUNE 21: [*Banks*] Roads better. Saw a pretty looking young woman walking, noticed her for several days. She walks a great deal and seems as little tired as any man. Our cattle nearly exhausted. A few evenings since saw eight boys playing, ages five to ten. It struck me a queer sight in this wilderness. This region still looks wild and barren. It possesses one blessing, good water. Saw some good springs. Crossed several clear streams. In the evening went a mile to get some buffalo meat. The poor fellow was chased seven miles, then fell in a small stream. They had carried nearly all of him away, but we took some good pieces. The long hair on his head and neck, often twelve to eighteen inches long, gives the buffalo a very wild and savage appearance. Got very tired. This day very fine. Distance fifteen miles.

JUNE 22: [*Banks*] Left camp five. Reached the Platte at noon. Prepared to cross the stream, ten feet to fifteen deep— and rapid. Six or eight men drowned and much cattle. Finally concluded to go up on this side. A great crowd trying to pass over on some rafts; others in wagon beds made tight.[11] This was our plan. One raft sells at twenty dollars; each person is pledged to sell at the same price. It is promised twenty-four hours ahead. Just now reported another man drowned. It seems a little like a battlefield. Encamped on Deer Creek, a pretty stream. Saw a specimen of the coal found in the bluffs near. It is excellent. Grass nearly all eaten. Sent our cattle two miles up the creek. The pasture good. A man accidently shot dead near this spot last evening. Weather delightful. Distance ten miles.

JUNE 23: [*Banks*] Remained in camp. Finally thought best to cross here. Expect to next morning. Caught some fine fish, enough for three meals for all. A blacksmith is hammering over the creek like vulcan. Offered fifteen dollars for shoeing a yoke of oxen. Mr. Drake made some shoes for our cattle. This day warm and cloudy.

JUNE 24: [*Banks*] Was on duty last night. Kept our cattle up creek all night. Slept part of the time on the grass with nothing between us and the clear blue sky. Left camp seven. Disappointed in our plans. Started for the Mormon ferry; hear the prospect good.[12] This morning Mr. Rose of Galliad and two men joined us with one wagon. Wonderful quantities of prickly pear in bloom. A sandy, barren soil is its home. Killed a rattle snake. The water in springs and runs as a general thing alkaline. Reeves well. He walked most of the day. Encamped on the Platte. Distance fifteen.

JUNE 25: [*Banks*] Clear and beautiful. In some places the ground is covered with grasshoppers, or sandhoppers, for there is very little grass. The earth seems baked. I have seen vast number of astonishingly large crickets. They are so fat they can scarcely get out of our way (the only thing fat here). Writers say the Indians eat them. We passed a slough so highly impregnated with alkali that six or eight oxen were laying near it. Some of our men brought in pure salaratus.[13] I shortly afterwards saw the dry bed of a slough white with same substance. It is dangerous to drink any water in this region except from the Platte. As I went to get water this morning I saw its bank white. The fires which have raged through this region are beyond the conception of man. We crossed the river without accident. The ferry is owned by two young men who think this is a rich foretaste of California. They charge two dollars for each wagon and you work it across yourself. The rope also you find by which it is drawn across; two yoke of oxen draw it on each side. It is formed by lashing three canoes together; fifty may cross in a day and the supply is great. No small specie. We saw a small rock standing on the roadside; it looks like a large fireplace. It's covered with names. I scratched my name. The road on this side is deep sand, scarcely enough grass for one ox, much less thousands. Encamped on the Platte. Distance ten miles.

JUNE 26: [Armstrong] *Left camp early in the morning. Drove about six miles and we left the river for Willow Springs, which is twenty-seven miles, the first afternooon.[14] Distance fifteen miles.*

[*Banks*] Left camp early. Roads very deep sand (this tires cattle) and grass all along the road very scattering. We have seen seven dead oxen this day and one cow too weak to stand. Saw a pond encrusted with salaratus, around the bank white as snow. We constantly watch that none of our cattle drink from any slough or run. It is thought the air contains alkali to such a degree that emigrants will not use milk in this neighborhood. I passed over the ashes of a volcano; there are some fifty mounds of rock thrown up in a boiling caldron. This evening cloudy, a raw wind from the snowclad mountains. This journey more than ever convinces me of the fallacy of Fourierism. Many are disposed to be authoritative, few to submit, and the interest of all seems to be the interest of none. We see large companies bursting into fragments, scarcely knowing wherefore. Encamped on the plain. Distance fifteen.

JUNE 27: [Armstrong] *Started for the Springs. Seen a great many dead cattle caused by drinking alkali which is very plenty through here. Got here about two in the afternoon. Took dinner and drove a short distance, which made the distance twenty miles.*

[*Banks*] Left camp six. I could almost say with the Queen of Sheba. The half was not told me. Saw valleys white with alkali; water encrusted, in some places red as any lye. In short, yesterday at noon we left the Platte; from that time to three o'clock this day (at which time we reached Willow Springs), though we saw much water we dared not use it for ourselves or cattle, except a mineral spring three miles east of the Willow Springs at which some of us drank. We crossed a small stream that we were aware to be poisonous. I washed my hands and face; it felt like lye. I expected to see dead cattle, but was astonished to find within the distance of eight or ten miles sixteen dead and one left as useless, eight of which I afterwards heard were killed by lightning. They lay side by side as they fell in their yokes. The owner soon had a team yoked up which was given him by the train to which he belonged. Many of them are bound to aid and assist each other to their journey's end. The water of Willow Springs is excellent and plentiful. Few places of business have the customers that they have. The roads this day good. In one place it passes through a narrow defile of rocks thrown up by volcanic action. There are seven or eight ranges of them like waves of the sea. Their length not more than one-fourth mile. I have many times seen sand in the distance appear like lakes or streams of pure water, a delusion often mentioned by travelers in this region. The earth has been uncommonly sterile this day. The sage can scarcely live. Encamped four miles west of Willow Springs. Grass middling in a valley near water so that we can use it. All are rushing for the Sweetwater twenty-seven miles ahead. Grass said to be good in that locality. Rained a heavy shower last night, heavier toward the mountains than with us. The roads have a firm crust today. Distance twenty miles.

JUNE 28: [Armstrong] *This day's drive very much like yesterday in respect to water and grass, and also a great many dead cattle. We crossed a small stream called Greasewood Creek. Distance eighteen miles.*

[Banks] This day's journey very much like yesterday. Alkali in abundance; some six or eight dead oxen, also one dead mule, another left. It is amusing to see men trying to bring on lame cattle. One will try for hours, then give up; another will try the game with the same effect, tiring themselves very much. We crossed Greasewood Creek at noon. Saw an Irish woman and daughter without any relatives on the way for gold. It is said she owns a fine farm in Missouri. We are encamped close to Independence Rock.[15] I have been on it and drank water in a cleft. It covers much ground but is not very high. The Sweetwater flows almost by its base. It is slightly alkaline. At noon the heat was great, now disagreeably cold. The mountains almost surround us. Grass tolerably good. Distance eighteen miles.

JUNE 29: [Armstrong] *Left Independence Rock. Drove but a short distance till we crossed Sweetwater River. The roads very sandy and hard wheeling. Drove to the Devil's Gate. It is a place where the river runs through the mountain.*[16] *It is about four hundred yards long and about sixty wide, and about three hundred high. Distance five miles.*

[Banks] Crossed the river without trouble. This day we found some of our cattle unable to travel. The mountains are rightly named; they are a mass of rocks. Occasionally in a chasm a cedar or pine finds soil enough to live. Philosophers say there is no such thing as innate beauty, preconceived ideas regulate all this. Be this as it may, who can gaze on the Sweetwater's passage through the mountains (called Devil's Gate) without feelings of the livest emotions? It is grand, it is sublime! Fifty feet of a chasm having perpendicular walls three hundred feet high yawning over the gulf below. He must be brainless that can see this unmoved. Here memory will dwell. Not much alkali seen today. We are reaching a high altitude. I never heard bullets whistle so in my life. I think this must be the cause. Saw about as many dead cattle this day as yesterday. Grass good for this road. This day traveled but little. Distance five miles. Encamped near Devil's Gate.

JUNE 30: [Armstrong] *Weather rather damp and cold for the time of the year. Grass very good. Drove off the road one mile to get it. Distance fourteen miles.*

[*Banks*] Out last night watching cattle. Left camp early to ascend the mountain. This I write as I stand on a remarkable spot. I have seen this almost miracle as I gazed upwards, but to stand on the topmost stone looking down into the deep, dark abyss, as I do now, language fails me. Look westward on the grassy plain encircled by snowcrest mountains, the beautiful Sweetwater meandering through its bosom, appearing like a chain of lakes, and you have part of the scene. Toward the rising sun you see rugged piles of massive rock and you stand awed. Last evening I stood here and saw a dozen campfires on the plain like the stars shining below, not above. I said goodbye, but now I give it salute. It sounds like thunder. Saw a lake three or four miles in circumference completely encrusted with pure salaratus. We see a dead ox almost every mile. We left our stoves this day; our teams failing. I almost fear for ourselves, but dread the consequences to the thousands behind. I hear of great suffering among teams. A little rain, evening cool. Mr. Shepard killed an antelope last evening. Roads bad. Distance seventeen miles.

JULY 1: [Armstrong] *Drove seven miles on the river and left, took over the mountains. Drove fourteen miles before dinner. We came to the river and we crossed the river three times in less than a half hour. Distance eighteen miles.*

[*Banks*] We have on this day [Sunday] traveled more or less ever since we left home. Many of the trains rest on this day, which makes the road less dusty and but little delay at difficult places, and furthers the opportunity of leaving many in our rear. For my part I would rest except under difficult circumstances. It seems a strange week that has no *Sunday*. We have traveled fast; few have done better. Passed through several narrow places in the mountains, one so narrow and difficult we had to cross the river twice. Our loads being heavy we wade the streams. Saw a girl who had written her name on a rock, Catherine Arnold. The rocks are in some places covered with names. Encamped on the Sweetwater. Distance eighteen miles.

JULY 2: [Armstrong] *We left one of our wagons and great many other things, and Mr. Paine left us this morning where we took dinner near a small valley where there was ice in abundance.*[17] *It was under the ground about six inches and the ice was about the same thickness. We have been in sight of snow three or four days, but do not appear to get any nearer. Encamped on Sweetwater River. Distance twenty-two miles.*

[*Banks*] Some strife of a very disagreeable nature. Here we left one of our wagons whole and sound. Our teams failed too much to bring it on. Saw two other wagons castaway, much property of other kinds, three stoves thrown away and three hundred pounds of bacon in one place. The number of dead oxen is such that should they increase in the same ratio they will create a pestilence. It is diseased. Saw large quantities of alkali today. Saw men getting ice in a valley. It is about five inches below the surface and nearly the like thickness. It is highly impregnated with saltpeter, which measurably accounts for its remaining this late in the season. The Wind River Mountains were in view most of this day. They are nearly covered by snow, an astonishing sight the 3rd of July. This day cold with very high wind. Roads deep sand. Paine and company left us in no very good humor. Encamped on Sweetwater River. Distance twenty-two miles.

JULY 3: [Armstrong] *Left camp early in the morning. Crossed the river and drove four miles, and crossed twice,* and took dinner. Yesterday we heard that there had been murder committed by a man by the name of Everette. He had formerly lived in Athens, Ohio. He murdered his partner and threw him in Platte River. We heard he was to be hanged. Distance eight miles.

[*Banks*] The grandeur of the snowclad mountains as the sun shone on them was dazzling. Heard a report yesterday which is confirmed now of a Mr. Everette, formerly of Athens, Ohio, having murdered his companion. They were traveling with pack mules. Some who had seen them on the road asked him of his friend. He answered he saw him drown in the Platte. They immediately took the rascal prisoner, previously having found the deceased pierced by a bullet. An Illinois train has charge of the prisoner. One report says he will be hung tomorrow at the Pacific Springs, some thirty-one miles west. Saw a brother-in-law of Hannegan's who says Hannegan told him the Whigs first nominated him to Prussia.[18] This day painfully cold, the wind blowing very hard from snowy peaks. Stopped most of this day to rest our cattle. Heard there is some two thousand teams before us, and not less than five thousand behind. The general health good. Distance eight miles.

JULY 4: [*Armstrong*] We can hear guns in all directions. The boys feel in pretty good spirits. We all loaded up our pieces. We gave our neighboring camps a few salutes, which made the old mountains ring. Here was a man who had been living in this part of the country for thirteen years. He has a family. He has been to the States only three times in the twelve years. This was on Sweetwater River. Drove from there to Strawberry Creek. We had good grass and water. Distance twelve miles.

[*Banks*] My Birthday! Thirty-one years since the

light first dawned on these eyes and I was folded in a parent's arms. Now for the first time absent on the return of this day. My breast heaves with emotion, but what are their thoughts? Would that I might know. Are they well? O thought forebear!

We ushered in this day with hearty salutes, but as we handled our guns we felt that Jack Frost was in company, though I had formerly understood Fourth of July a mortal enemy of his. Here the old fellow was in full uniform, nearly one-fourth of an inch thick. Our dinner was a grand affair, all things considered. Some good stewed gooseberries, peach and apple pies, sweet cakes, and a noble appetite for sauce. Goodbye Fourth of July, you passed as a strange day to me! Encamped on Strawberry Creek. Grass good. Saw a man who had been thirteen years living in this wild; formerly of Missouri. Distance twelve miles.

JULY 5: [Armstrong] *Left camp about seven o'clock and we came on a short distance and came to a small stream where there was snowbanks that was from ten to fifteen feet deep. I was on one myself that was about that depth. It was quite solid. It is nothing strange to see snow here on the mountains. We are camped on Sweetwater. We leave it tomorrow for good. Distance fourteen miles.*

[*Banks*] Yesterday we ascended some five or six hundred feet over stony roads until we reached a plateau (in fact the top of the Rocky Mountains). Here the road is good. Such is the altitude of this part that there is snow in many of the valleys, always on the south side of the hill, which is caused by the northwest wind drifting it in vast heaps. This day I was walking on one which is from fifteen to sixteen feet in depth; others also very large, probably in the high part of the mountains near us not less than one hundred feet in the deepest place. The water is icy cold. A grave near us: Mr. Estell of Missouri, fifty years old. Saw one at Independence Rock: Mr. Fulkerson, aged eighteen, died in 1845. Grass rather poor. Encamped on Sweetwater of which we lose sight tomorrow. Evening cool. Distance eleven.

South Pass to the Humboldt

July 6—August 8

[After paralleling the Platte to the junction of its two principal branches, the Buckeye gold-seekers followed the South Fork only a short distance before crossing over to the North Fork. They followed the latter stream for two weeks, stopping briefly at Fort Laramie, before turning to the Sweetwater and South Pass. A fast pace and overladened wagons took a heavy toll of teams during the ascent of the Rocky Mountains.]

JULY 6: [Armstrong] *Crossed Sweetwater for the last time. Drove eight miles. We drove off the road to the Sweetwater to noon, which was within half a mile of the Oregon line. The line is on the summit of the mountains. We drove about two miles apast the Pacific Springs and camped. Distance fourteen miles.*

[Banks] Oregon Territory. Here I am and the Rocky Mountains between me and home. Started half past six, forded Sweetwater the seventh or eighth time. Walked over a bed of snow ten feet deep. Snow was uncommonly heavy last winter, the spring cold and late. I suppose this scene is uncommon. We gradually ascended until noon. We took dinner on the banks of the Sweetwater, even here a considerable stream. A short time after we left we heard men cheering; we were through the pass! Until now the waters on which we camp and those that pass my home mingle in one common flood as they roll toward the Atlantic; here they seek the Pacific's tide. Everyday (for a few days) the wind rises about eleven a.m., and blows hard the rest of the day. The air is so cold in the mountains that when the atmosphere is warm on the plains it rushes in. Some frost last night.

This morning a colored boy some nine or ten years old was driving a team when he was run over by a heavy wagon, one wheel passing over his face, the other over his chest. He is expected to recover. I had seen him playing in the morning; such is life. Saw some men whose mules were lost; they gave them up and ceased hunting them. The road on this side is good. Passed the Pacific Springs, fine water. The earth for a considerable distance is boggy, shaking at every step. Encamped two miles below on a small stream. Distance fourteen miles.

JULY 7: [Armstrong] *Left camp pretty early. Six miles to Dry Sandy. From here we drove two miles apast it and nooned. We drove to Little Sandy. The roads was very dusty. We passed the Salt Lake road which is about four miles from the creek. We camped on the bank of the creek. Distance nineteen.*

[*Banks*] Saw the colored boy; he is better. His master and mistress seem kind. Saw Vinyard, who killed a man in the Wisconsin legislature some years since.[1] He appears a saucy, ignorant, unprincipled man. Saw an individual who left St. Joseph later than we did. He says not less than a thousand persons have died on the road. The cholera has been more fatal among the Missourians than others (this seems to be the general opinion); the cause assigned intemperance and uncleanliness. Since leaving the Platte the general health has been good. My health since I left home has been excellent. I am the only one of the company who has not been more or less sick. On the fifth, Messrs. Shepard and H. L. Graham killed two antelopes, the flesh of which is delicious. Today we have three sage, or mountain, hens and a hare for dinner. The hare is the same as the European. Sage is almost the only wood of very much of this route. It grows from one to seven feet high, having a stalk sometimes four or five inches in diameter. We intend to take Sublette's Cutoff.[2] Such is the anxiety to go ahead that thirty-five miles without water weighs but little against the additional time of the other road, that being seventy-five miles longer. Not less than one hundred wagons encamped near us. Encamped on the Little Sandy. Distance nineteen miles.

JULY 8: [Armstrong] *We started for Big Sandy which is five miles from Little Sandy. We took Sublette's Cutoff. We left the main road to our left; between those two rivers the road takes off. We crossed Sandy and went about one mile and camped. We laid there from ten o'clock Sunday [July 8] till five p.m. We was resting our cattle for a forty-mile stretch. Distance six miles.*

[*Banks*] Started for Big Sandy. Encamped on its bank. Distance six miles. Here we intend to remain until Monday evening when we cross the desert. Saw some shoeing horses all day, others playing cards. Much of the forms and seriousness of this world is merely following bellwethers. We feel very much inclined to follow the crowd. Big and Little Sandy has water much the same as the Platte; slightly alkaline and muddy.

JULY 9: [Armstrong] *We started for Green River, which is forty miles without water or much grass. We started at five p.m. and we got to Green River at four p.m. the next day.*

We stopped at eleven o'clock that night and let the cattle graze about an hour, and then drove till four in the morning. We drove the balance of the trip without stopping. The cattle very nearly exhausted. We tried to swim our cattle but could not make any of them swim.

[*Banks*] Out with cattle last night in Mr. Barnes' place (he is sick). S. Townshend and I slept two miles from camp without arms. The Indian traders have all the property left by emigrants at their own disposal. They tell the Indians to beware of cholera and smallpox. The country appears sterile, yet there is very good grass growing in tufts. A heap of tenacious sand near us we call the Hay Stack, which it resembles. Paine's folks a day ahead; Jenkins' nearly a week behind. By some falling back and others going rapidly onward we often hear news. Nothing definite as regards Everette. Some say he is taken to Fort Hall to receive trial. Our cattle are improving. A hard night near both for them and us.

JULY 10: [*Armstrong*] *We tried to swim them* [cattle] *again, but did not get but three head over.*

[*Banks*] Started last evening at five p.m. Traveled until eleven, rested an hour, traveled on till four p.m. this day. It is a dismal journey, most of the time dust three or four inches deep and wind blowing. I was driving loose stock and toward the end of our march became very much exhausted; had to lay down to rest several times. When I would raise my head I felt faint, my mouth burning with thirst. Within one-half mile of Green River (which seemed to me to be receding as we advanced) I found a spring of pure appearance though surrounded by alkali. I drank and felt much refreshed. I had never felt so prostrated in my life. All were fatigued, some nearly as much as myself. Two nights' loss of rest and driving made my lot the hardest. I cannot forget this dreary and desolate land. Encamped on Green River, a rapid, turbulent stream one hundred and fifty yards wide. Distance by roadometer forty-one miles.[3]

JULY 11: [Armstrong] *We tried again [to get our cattle across] till noon. We only got seven head more over, then we came to the conclusion to swim them by the side of a skiff, which we had to pay two dollars for the use of it to swim eleven head over. The Mormons have a ferry here.[4] It crosses the Green River. They charge four dollars per wagon. They ferry from fifty to sixty wagons a day.*

[Banks] Tried last evening to swim our cattle; to-day tried again. Got a few over. The stream is so rapid they dread it. Got our wagons ferried over at four dollars each. The ferry is owned by Mormons. While others are chasing wealth they are catching it, no dream. For the use of a skiff to swim our cattle half a day, two dollars. Money but little and property of no value. This evident on every side.

JULY 12: [Banks] Tried to get our cattle over again. Was in the water three hours. Very cold, the snow melting makes it icy cold. The last time I thought to force them across. I went to the middle of the river. I had a hard pull to reach shore. We gave up and had to bring them over as above named. A hard day for all. My skin burns from exposure to the sun. Upwards of fifty wagons daily pass. The noise is incessant. Salt Lake less than two hundred miles. There are a number of Frenchmen here who have squaws for wives. They call themselves traders, but I never have seen gambling equal to what I saw in one of their wigwams. I never despised human nature as I now do. I see many having no claim to humanity but form. Many of the emigrants are talented, high-minded men. The Granville Company have some such. Take the aggregate, they are woefully in the minority, but take the same number in many states and the comparison would be in favor of the former. I find a large amount of Mexican volunteers on this route, but as I formerly remarked a good spirit pervades the most.

JULY 13: [Armstrong] *Still at the ferry.*

[*Banks*] Last night I could scarcely sleep; I felt so exceedingly sore. We will remain here this day to recruit our cattle. They are failing very much. One is so far gone we left him on the other side; two we had to pull out of the river. Trouble stares us yet, we hope for the best. A Mr. Cary of Wisconsin let us have a yoke of fine oxen for taking some one hundred and fifty pounds for him. He is packing. Hundreds are leaving wagons, throwing away all but what they can pack. The weather fine for many days.

JULY 14: [Armstrong] *We leave the ferry this morning. The roads very dusty and hilly. We seen four graves today, more than I have seen for a great many days. Put our cattle out at noon. Going to stay till morning. Camped on a small stream called Camp Creek. Distance eight miles.*

[*Banks*] Again moving. Saw four graves; three men, one woman, Mary, consort of J. M. Fulkerson, date 1847. He lost son and wife on this (to him) sad journey.[5] More sickness now than since we left the Platte. The mountain air is too pure for their lungs, giving coughs and in some cases fever. It seems strange that which is vigor to the healthy should be death to the weakly. I have said all kinds of property were thrown away. Who ever saw whiskey thrown away? No one on this road, except throwing it down a drunkard's neck be throwing it away, the way which all they can possibly come at goes, diluted alcohol (bought expecting to burn it), or anything to be crazy. Last night the Irish woman and daughter were selling liquor near us, and such cursing and swearing, quarreling and bragging it has seldom been my misfortune to hear. Fifty cents a pint, quite moderate. Saw some Indian French carry off the comfort. The Indians show themselves a little on this side of Green River. This whole region is a miserable, dreary waste. Lofty mountains and dashing torrents make the sum of its attractions. You seldom see a bird, and he can scarcely warble for sadness. Civilization may make roads or plant cities, but the country can be fit for none other than wandering savages. On the streams you sometimes find grass, the upland has little vegetation and that covered by swarms of mosquitoes ready to devour the weary traveler who can find no shade except a great rock. Encamped on a stream six miles from the ferry. Grass good.

JULY 15: [Armstrong] *Sunday morning. Left camp pretty early. The roads very hilly and dusty. We drove about two miles up the creek and crossed, left the creek to our right hand, drove about two miles from the creek and came to a small run where there was good water. After we left there the water was plenty. We are camped at a place where there is good spring water. There was a man shot himself this morning near us with a shotgun. Shot through the foot. It happened by pulling the gun out of the wagon muzzel foremost. Distance sixteen miles.*

[Banks] Sunday. I know it by counting this day to Sunday next, following the last day of the week, otherwise I should not know it. Today dusty and hilly, tolerably well watered. This of all days calls my mind most forcibly to home. At noon my spirit seemed to be there, but it returned to mourn my absence. Encamped nearly on the mountain again. Distance sixteen miles.

JULY 16: [Armstrong] *Left camp early this morning. Traveled over a very hilly country, the worst hills we have traveled over yet. Very stony. The springs very plenty and the water cold. Grass very plenty and the best quality. There was a very fine shower today about noon, the first rain we have had for several weeks. We are camped on Ham's Fork of Bear River. The distance from Camp Creek to this stream is about thirty miles. We have been in sight of snow for the last four weeks. Distance sixteen miles.*

[*Banks*] Saw what aroused my sympathies much; a man wayworn and weary, upwards of forty-five years of age, his countenance indicating debility, journeying solitary and alone with some forty pounds of provisions on his back. We asked him to breakfast with us. He left home having a horse which died a few miles this side of St. Joseph. That place he left on the seventeenth of May, having walked nearly all this long journey. He leaves a family. The road is mountainous. Now you are on a high mountain and snow lower down than you; presently in a valley crossing a dashing stream, then raise your eyes and view the track, see now it winds, sometimes almost rearing up, then falling until it gains the summit of yonder mountain. This is our road. Water plenty and good. Soil much better, grass also good. Encamped on Thomas Ham's Fork of Bear River. Distance sixteen miles.

JULY 17: [Armstrong] *We leave Ham's Fork of Bear River for the main stream which is twenty-eight miles and a very mountainous country, worse than any roads we have traveled. We camped on a small stream which was made altogether by springs. It was the finest kind of water. Distance fifteen.*

[*Banks*]   Left camp half past five. Climb is the first part of our drive this morning. The parts of the mountains we travel is a kind of tableland. Today it is rich in soil and grass, covered by a beautiful blue flower of a large growth of flax, differing in no respect (that I could see) from that raised by Ohio farmers. Two graves this day, one on the fourth instant, the other Mrs. Mary Campbell, died July 16, 1846. The Wind River Mountains in sight. They are more grand from this than the other side; they are equal to my former thoughts of the Rocky Mountains. The clouds seem to repose on their summits and the snow to find a resting place. We climb a mountain this morning that seemed as if it never would find the summit, but of all the going down hill I have ever seen or heard of, this beat in two miles not less than between two and three thousand feet. Both hind wheels locked and even then we had to hold to the wagon. It is so exceedingly steep as to be painful to walk down. Encamped in a beautiful fertile vale delightfully watered at the foot of the mountain. Distance fifteen miles.

JULY 18: [Armstrong] *Left the camp about six o'clock. Drove over a tremendous hill which was about four miles over in about six miles from where we started. We took dinner near a fine spring. We drove on about four miles farther and we came to Thomas' Fork of Bear Creek. We crossed over. It was considered one of the swiftest streams we have crossed yet. It empties into the main river a few rods from where we crossed. We are camped here now. Distance ten miles.*

[*Banks*] Our march this day very similar to yesterday's, only not quite so bad. The soil is of a limestone quality. Saw a large flax today, as large as I have ever seen, though I have seen what is considered uncommon. Nooned in sight of Bear River. Traveled up it some miles, crossed Thomas' Fork; it is some ninety feet wide, three feet deep, current like a mill-tail. It plainly tells its origins. Saw a chap who has some knowledge of rodomontade; said he was very fond of traveling, thought this trip cured him. Saw many of the States, traveled in England and France, looked rather green. Said his home was near Dayton and acquainted with none but leading characters. I asked him if he had not been a sailor; he left. I saw three graves this day; five of those I saw yesterday and today were females, dating since one or two years back. Oregon emigrants I presume. I often heard their trials were great, but this year will tell a sadder tale of woe. Evening grand. Love never dwelt in a much more charming valley. Here one might live secluded. From side to side his eyes might rest on mountain tops and no gate left open, except where the babbling waters play. Poor fellow, I have not seen his fair one yet! I don't think I should envy him. Encamped on Bear. Distance twelve.

JULY 18: [6] [Armstrong] *This morning we start up a small stream to get across. We was camped near where it emptied into Bear River. We came pretty nearly back to where we started from. We had to leave the river on account of the canyon. It came down to the water's edge. It was six miles across. Distance twelve miles.*

JULY 19: [Armstrong] *Left camp [word missing] past. We keep down Bear River. The roads very good and grass the same. The night very cold. We are scarcely out of sight of snow. Bear River is about two hundred feet wide and very deep, the bottoms quite wide, and in some places the soil is pretty good, and others very thin. Distance twelve.*

[*Banks*] Left camp one quarter of five. Traveled on a good road up Bear River. It is a fine stream. I swam across. It is about two hundred feet wide, deep, and cold. Here the days are hot, the nights on the contrary are cold. Night before last we had some frost. We are scarcely out of sight of snow at any time. We are now on the main road once more. Encamped on the north bend of Bear, about one hundred miles from Fort Hall.⁷ Traveling slowly. All our neighbors passing us. Our cattle improving. Distance twelve miles.

JULY 20: [Armstrong] *Traveled but little in the forenoon; the afternoon the roads very bad, dusty, and hilly. The dust was two to six inches deep. We leave the river on account of a canyon; the rocks come down to the water's edge. Have got two or three days' travel down wrong side. Distance twelve.*

[*Banks*] Traveled but little in the forenoon. In the afternoon the roads like the world—worse and worse. The circuit around the canyon of Bear River is at one time in a deep ravine, presently on the top of a mountain. The mountain you descend at the river is perhaps two thousand feet high, covered by dust three to six inches deep, torn by the locking of wheels. I am astonished how men ever found a passage through these rugged piles of rock and earth.

"Truth is strange, stranger than fiction." Mrs. Jenkins and Mr. Lancaster, being desirous to rid themselves of Mr. Jenkins, induced Henry B. Lancaster and John Chase to shoot him; the former to be rewarded by the hand of Alice Jenkins, the latter to have a daughter of Lancaster's. Lancaster, a preacher, a son of a mason, and a lawyer, failed in his nefarious plans. Young Lancaster and Chase inveigled Jenkins from the road pretending they had seen gold. They fired, he staggered and fell, as they thought never to rise. They ran at the top of their speed yelling, "Indians, Indians." As soon as the old man saw they were gone he went to a Kentucky camp, soothed his wounds, and told his sad tale. Lancaster missed, but Chase, who had Jenkins' own shotgun loaded with buckshot, lodged the load in poor Jenkins' neck. He is recovering and on his way for California. Judas' counterpart is with him; for his family's sake he lets her remain with them until he arrives in California.[8] Chase was not caught; old and young Lancaster were tried and sentenced to return to the States, and if caught on the road or in California they will be shot. The Oregon troops would take them to Oregon if witnesses would accompany them. This being refused, so the villains are at large. Strange to say, Alice was inconsolable for the loss of her lover. O Shame, where is thy blush? The old watery-eyed scoundrel left a wife and family in Illinois. Weather fine. Distance fifteen miles.

JULY 21: [Armstrong] *Saw an Indian encampment. Drove but a short distance. We traded two oxen for one to a Mormon that was living a trading with the emigrants. There was several Frenchmen that has been with them twenty-two years. It is the Snake Indians. There was an old squaw that owned ninety horses. Distance fourteen.*

[Banks] Saw an Indian encampment of the Snake Nation. Some of the men are fine looking. One was a complete coxcomb; tall, and handsome, his face shining with vermilion, his long hair beautifully combed and parted in the middle, some of his locks rolled in brass and red flannel, a coarse comb ornamented his right cheek, and pleasure marked his countenance. A fine grey blanket completely enveloped his form and moccasins. Get out of the way broadway dandies! The belle was attired in dressed buffalo's skin made

like a lady's mantua on her back; for a mantilla was an antelope skin dressed with the hair on, quite fine. The head chief
of the Nation is not ostentatious; a red shirt, a bunch of brass
trinkets on his left wrist, and a red string around an old hat
mark his majesty. His swordbearer carries a sword and a piece
of red cloth woven with feathers. I saw some of them moving;
the squaw done all the work, packed the horses, fastened the
tent poles as shafts, and off they went. A young papoose
about three years old went around shaking hands and saying,
"how do, how do." They seem to live comfortably (for Indians), their horses are numerous and excellent. Here are
some French mountaineers trading, also a Mormon and his
wife trading in lame cattle, moccasins, whiskey piss, and company. We traded two lame for one not very sound ox, yet a
good bargain. The Mormons are alive to any means of acquir-
ing wealth. The road this day on the river bottom. It is good.
Distance fourteen miles.

The first train which passed this place was drawn by oxen.
They were from Iowa and New York. Captain Stewart passed
June 20th, so says the Mormon.[9]

JULY 22: [Armstrong] *A fine morning, though rather warm.
We was camped on a fine little stream. It was from ten to
fifteen feet wide, the water came from springs. There they
don't run more than two or three miles. There is quite a number of them through this part of the country. There was a fine
shower this afternoon which helps the traveling; the dust was
so deep that it was disagreeable. Camped early near a spring.
Distance ten miles.*

[Banks] Fine, though rather warm. Mosquitoes
very annoying. The afternoon hard showers and high winds,
the clouds resting on the mountains. Two graves this day;

the first that of Mr. Lamb of the neighborhood of St. Joseph. He leaves a wife and six children. Mr. Shepard unwell; all others of the company well. Man has much to remind him of his mortality and direct his mind to matters of vital importance, but cursing, swearing, and profanity is the order of the day, not merely here, but wherever man is. We daily see man is opposed to truth; sunken as he is, he thinks to fit himself for purity. I often hear this argument. They have no care for mercy and only mercy; Christ died to save and did save. They spurn, but to those who hear His words, He is precious. It is finished. Now it is clear and cold. Yet on Bear River. Distance ten miles.

JULY 23: [Armstrong] *We commenced traveling a little farther in a day. For the last week or ten days we have been recruiting our cattle. We traveled ten miles before noon. Went out a squirrel hunting. I killed eighteen in traveling ten miles. We are camped near the Steamboat Spring, three miles from the Beer Spring.*[10] *There is several beer springs near us. We passed two or three of the greatest springs. I went to one spring to get a drink; it boiled up out of a rock in more than fifty places at the head of the spring. It was ten feet wide; half a mile below it was forty feet wide. We came to an encampment of the Snake Indians. Four miles from here there is a cutoff which goes between Fort Hall and Salt Lake road, which is said to cut off from eighty to one hundred and twenty miles, but we don't know whether we will take it or not.*[11] *There was not any wagons gone this route till four days ago. We have taken the cutoff. It is thirteen miles to water from the forks of the road. The road is good and grass the same. Distance seventeen.*

[*Banks*] Commenced today to travel farther, delaying serves our cattle but wastes our stock of provisions.

Between lightening our loads and short drives we may run short. Saw some Indians. They are sprightly and happy, at least in appearance, but such a life. Women robed in dirty leather wandering about with a papoose strapped on their backs. Begging food from everyone they see may have charm for them. Children six to eight years old naked and at the same employment as their mothers. And their fathers, noble fellows, an old shirt or vest, a pair of moccasins, and a blanket and they are rigged. A horse and a gun, our hero is as proud as one of Napoleon's Legion of Honor. They eat lice. In the forenoon I felt it difficult to breathe, a sensation I have not much felt before. My spirits were low till I heard, "There is the Soda Springs." This acted like electricity, but when I drank I thought more poetry than truth. The Beer Springs I feared would be so. Such is not the case; they are wonderful and deserve a place in the wonders of the earth. I have drank small beer not much better. There are many springs. They foam and blubber and are as busy as a brewhouse. The gas is constantly escaping. The temperature low, and the quantity such from the Soda and Beer Springs as to make a large creek in the distance of two miles. We are surely on strange ground, within the Great Basin, surrounded by lofty mountains. All its waters flow to the Salt Lake (the Dead Sea of this continent), there to remain until drawn toward the sky again to fall and renew its course. A few years since all was still except the whoop of the red man; now five thousand civilized beings dwell near the lake. A few years and this valley may hum with busy life. Such is the history of this Nation. Encamped on Bear. Distance seventeen.

JULY 24: [Armstrong] *We leave the Beer Springs this morning for the cutoff; four miles to it. We got to it at eleven o'clock. We take it thirteen miles to the first water. It is a fine little stream. It comes out of the mountains. It is very good water. Distance seventeen.*

[Banks] As soon as I waked this morning I went to a beer spring and could scarcely realize where I was. My mind was filled with the most solemn emotions; from nature my thoughts went up to the Creator of all things. View this district in every light, it is wonderful. The earth rings with a hollow sound and water is gushing out on all sides. The Steamboat Spring is sublimely grand. Its name is altogether appropriate, a never ceasing splashing of the wheel. It is on the bank of Bear River, yet its water is rather warmer than tepid. A rock formed by the deposits of this mineral beer covers much of the surface for miles. This day closed with wonders. The earth, as if weary under her burden, has sunk in hundreds of places. Some deep basins, others chasms fifteen or twenty feet deep, two or three feet wide; this in mighty granite I know not how deep. A plain about eight miles wide is everywhere marked by the footprints of a mighty earthquake. One or two extinguished volcanoes are yet visible. Here we take Lawson's Cutoff saving seventy-five miles, leaving Fort Hall on the right about sixty miles.[12] Saw a man riding an ox; queer sights on this road. Encamped on a small stream. Distance seventeen miles.

JULY 25: [Armstrong] *This morning we start up a very large mountain. It is covered with green service berries. The roads are good. Only six miles to the next creek, and four to the next. The two first were small; the latter is quite deep. I do not know the names of those creeks. We only drove five miles in the afternoon. Camped near a small stream. Distance fifteen miles.*

[Banks] The road good, though mountainous. The

number of roads the emigrants are taking is very fortunate. It will prevent much suffering. Saw a great many Indians. Distance eighteen miles.

JULY 26: [Armstrong] *We leave pretty early. Drove about seven miles and came to a small stream. We filled our canteens with water and drove three miles farther and took dinner. We drank all of the water out of them, and there was an Indian came to our camp and we asked him how far it was to water. He made signs that we would travel all that day and part of the night and, as bad luck would have it, the signs came true. We traveled on till eleven o'clock at night but found no water. When we stopped we heard there was water from two to three miles up in the mountain. We started; some got it and some did not. I never was so dry in my life, and I never seen so many thirsty men and cattle in my life. Distance twenty miles.*

[*Banks*] The days delightful but rather warm; the nights cold, and the last three frosty. Grass and water good, timber scarce. Sometimes we see small groves of cottonwood nearly all dead, which seems to be caused by fire. Willows are our principal fuel. The streams are small, pure, and rapid, generally at intervals of five to ten miles. The country a continued series of mountains. We are near Salt Lake. Roads good. Distance fifteen miles.

JULY 27: [Armstrong] *We leave very early, just at the dawn of day. We have twelve miles to water yet. The roads very dusty. Nights very cold, frost for several mornings. They are very frequent in this part of the country. We got to water about ten a.m. We lay here till morning. It is a fine spring. Distance twelve.*

[*Banks*] James' birthday; youngest, wildest, merriest, and I am afraid craziest of nine. I would like to see what he is doing on this his sixteenth birthday, but I cannot. Here this is a beautiful day. A constant wind cools the air, though it covers us with dust. This is only the seventh day since this road was traveled by wagons and ox teams, yet the road is deep and dusty in many places. Today, not knowing the nature of the road ahead, we took no water in our keg, which proved a sad mistake. Traveled until dark. Distance twenty miles.

JULY 28: [*Banks*] Last night went two miles up the mountains in search of water. Some of our men found a small spring of good water though we were told the point near which it was, it was difficult to find. We were very much exhausted. We came down one mountain yesterday which capt all others; steep, rough, and dust almost insupportable for a distance of two miles. This stretch is twenty-five miles. Encamped on a small stream in full view of the thirsty mortals rushing down to water. Just heard Jenkins had died of his wounds. Awful! Distance twelve miles.

JULY 29: [Armstrong] *We take up the line of march as usual and the day is pleasant. The roads are good and the best mountain roads we have had, and water in several places. We broke an axeltree just as we started down a ravine. We drove on till night, and we cut a pine tree in the morning, and by eleven o'clock we was ready to start. We drove. Distance sixteen miles.*

[*Banks*] A beautiful morning. The clearness of the mountain atmosphere is astonishing. Our day's travel has been constantly in the mountains, in one deep ravine, strange to say, nearly level. Several springs of good water refresh the dusty traveler; his ideas of the beautiful here may be gratified. In a gap of the mountains grandly curved he sees a grand amphitheatre formed by a large mountain gracefully rising behind, at the foot of which stand five or six pine trees. Toward evening we saw one of our axels giving way; must make a new one of pine. "Necessity has no law." Though the grass and water of this part of Oregon would seem to indicate game we have seen none except sage hens and ground squirrels. The latter do not much resemble the squirrel of the East; his tail is short and his belly disproportionately large. They are much eaten. I don't like them very well. Encamped on a small stream. Distance sixteen.

JULY 30: [Armstrong] *At work on the axeltree. By eleven o'clock we were ready to start. We kept down a small stream till it sank. There we camped till twelve tonight. Distance six miles.*

[Banks] First motion this morning was to make the axel. Some thought we might move from this place by nine a.m., but we found noon came before we were ready. Bought some bacon at four cents per pound, and flour at a little over three cents per pound; they had no pay for their trouble. Saw some days since a Charles Cox who was in Albany last winter hunting fugitives. William Wilson and Dr. Dixon immediately recognized him. William sung a song composed by Mr. Day for his benefit. We continued down the stream. We encamped on it till it sinks as it does entirely in the sand. The next stretch we hear is twenty-five miles without water. Here we remain till twelve p.m., then travel until noon tomorrow, at which time we expect to be through. A large mountain on our left about three miles distant overlooks the Salt Lake; it is some thirty or forty miles. I am afraid I would pay too dearly for the whistle if I went. Distance six miles.

JULY 31: [Armstrong] *We leave camp at twelve o'clock at*

night for a twenty-mile stretch. The roads were good. No moon in the latter part of the night. We got to Raft River about seven in the morning. We laid here till three in the afternoon, and then we drove over to the Fort Hall road, which was six miles from the place where we nooned. There was a great many camps. Distance twenty-one.

[*Banks*] We left camp at twelve last night. The plain over which we traveled is a desert, scarcely any vegetation except sage. Three or four of us whiled away the time by telling stories. About nine this morning, contrary to expectations, we found water. Our minds being engaged did not prevent our feet from making time. I was much tired. Saw a man who says no less than a thousand emigrants have passed from time to eternity. One company of twenty-five lost twenty-three. Encamped in sight of the Fort Hall road. Distance thirteen miles. From the sink in the evening we went six miles farther. It is very difficult to know how much we gained by the cutoff; some say seventy-five or eighty, others twenty or even less, our road however being better. We feel puzzled to know our locality. We are here but do not know where here is.

AUGUST 1: [*Armstrong*] *We came to the Fort Hall road this morning. We keep up Raft River for some dozen or ten miles. We are pretty near the head of it. At noon we left the river, then we drove over a very dry ridge which was seven or eight miles without water. At night we came to a small run that affords plenty of water. It comes from a snowbank. Distance sixteen.*

[*Banks*] Left camp early. Roads good, country rather barren. Heard no water ahead for many miles; again deceived, but this sort of deception is not so annoying as the other. All it does is make us carry a keg of water we otherwise would not. An eccentric Englishman by the name of Cooper has traveled with us some days. He is quite intelligent and rather agreeable. Some of our men unwell in consequence of loss of rest. My ankles pained so much I could not walk to-day. Grass good. Distance sixteen miles.

AUGUST 2: [Armstrong] *We keep down this run for three miles. We came to some alkali springs. Shortly after we left the alkali springs we came to a fine little creek; near that the Salt Lake road came into the other road. We found water plenty at noon. I seen one of the greatest sights that I most ever did see. It was rocks that stood very thick, different sizes from ten to one hundred feet high. We came over several large mountains. We camped in a valley. There was springs that afforded water for us and our cattle. Distance twenty.*

[*Banks*] Those who went by Salt Lake are daily coming into this road, that being impracticable even for pack mules. In some places it is a complete marsh. The Mormons are reported to be very friendly. In every grade of life, from the monarch on his throne to the savage lord of the wilderness, man is the children of circumstances, and a creature subject to strange vicissitudes of fortune. A few days since I saw an Indian of the Snake Nation returning to the home of his father after an absence of more than twenty years. When only four years old the Comanches stold him from his parents. He now returns, perhaps but to mark the waste of years. Child of nature, how your heart must have throbbed as you drew near your former home! Roads good, the face of the country picturesque. Saw some rocks of white, beautiful marble. In some places the rocks are exceedingly rugged and wild, evidently the work of some powerful convulsion. Some of our men saw a spring of hot water. I was not aware of it until we passed. Saw a deserter going to Fort Hall. Poor fellow, he did not feel very comfortable! Saw a grave; death by consumption. Encamped on a small stream. Distance twenty-one miles.

AUGUST 3: [Armstrong] *We start with the expectation of bad roads. It is very rough country. We find the road as expected, the worst road we have seen yet. We came down a very bad hill; there we found a fine run of water. We started for Goose Creek, which is four miles. Just as we got down onto Goose Creek we broke the axeltree that we put in a few days ago. We got it out of the wagon and in a few minutes a man came along with an extra one, and we bought it, paid one dollar. Distance twelve miles.*

[Banks] Our journey this day very uneven and difficult. On every side we see rugged mountains, the prospect very wild. We nooned near Goose Creek where as report has it two hundred men are digging gold with good success.[13] If so, we are near the shining metal. This afternoon our pine axel broke. Fortunately we bought an old one of a man who had picked it up, a dollar. A good bargain for us. Luckily we were near good camping on Goose Creek. Distance fifteen miles.

AUGUST 4: [Armstrong] *We leave camp about eleven o'clock. We got the wagon fixed and ready to start. Just as we got the cattle yoked, D. L. Dana came up.[14] He was packing. We traveled down Goose Creek and camped on grass and water. Distance fifteen miles.*

[Banks] This part of the route between Fort Hall and Mary's River is little spoken of by travelers. It is rather uninviting, though it has its curiosities, one of which is its warm springs. Saw Indians; beggary is their trade. Some of them are willing to trade anything they possess, except their ponies. They place a high value on food and powder and lead; from a quart to a half a peck of beans will buy a first-rate buffalo robe. A few charges of powder will purchase a pair of moccasins, and they are very fond of procuring clothing from the whites, and feel fine in their new costume. I bought a robe, a dollar, from a white (he gave a few beans for it) worth four to five dollars in St. Louis. Roads good. Grass also good. Encamped on Goose Creek. Distance seventeen miles.

AUGUST 5: [Armstrong] *Sunday morning. We left camp early. Still traveling down a valley. We came to some hot springs shortly after we started. It was as hot as common dishwater. It is said there is two hundred men a digging gold on this creek. We passed a small stream run after we left Goose Creek. We leave it to the right after we leave here. This last run is fourteen miles to the next water. Distance twenty-five.*

[Banks] Saw some warm springs in one of which I bathed. The water was painfully warm at first; in a few minutes it seemed agreeable. I remained in twenty or thirty minutes. Felt some lassitude the rest of the day. Saw small caves in rocks like sentry boxes; the stone is soft inside. They are covered by names. In one I cut my name. Shortly afterwards in another I saw Ino Banks, Virginia. I felt surprised. We traveled late over a barren plain. About eight o'clock we came to a small creek formed by a spring. No grass; a hard prospect for our cattle. This has been a hard day's drive. Distance twenty-six miles.

AUGUST 6: [Armstrong] *We got to Hot Spring Valley last night.[15] Here is a fine spring of good cool water. We travel* down this valley, and the valley is forty miles long. This day Dr. Dixon and D. L. Dana start to go on to the diggins to look out a situation for the company. They left. We took dinner at a very fine spring. The water sinks in the creek and it is difficult to get water without digging in the bed of the creek some three or four feet. We are camped near one of those holes. Distance fourteen miles.

[Banks] Very contradictory stories of grass and water. Some say six miles to water, the next twenty-four miles. Dr. Dixon intends to push on as fast as possible in advance of us so as to gain all necessary information and meet us so that we may have an advantageous location to drive to. A great desideratum. He is accompanied by Daniel Dana of Athens. They left in the afternoon. We elected William Logan captain *ad interim*. A few drops of rain. This climate is wonderfully dry. No dew; the earth like ashes, except near water. Encamped on good grass. No water, only by digging in the bottom of the run. Distance fifteen miles.

AUGUST 7: [Armstrong] We continue downstream. Yet pleasant, but rather cold. Quite a heavy frost last night. Days warm; rather singular kind of weather. Trains pretty thick. We traveled about eight miles in the forenoon. About one mile west of the road good springs. It is quite dusty today. The wind blows hard. Distance eighteen miles.

[Banks] Roads good; a matter of great importance to us. Water difficult to procure, but occasionally we find a little in deep holes of an almost dried up creek. Captain Cooper left. "Go ahead" his motto. We are not fast enough for him. Encamped on Warm Creek. Distance sixteen miles.

AUGUST 8: [Armstrong] Camped on a run that is quite warm. I think the hot springs must be at the head of it. We are going to try to get to one branch of Mary's River, or Humboldt as it is called.[16] We have got to Mary's River, at the head springs of it. We are camped at the springs. Fine grass and water. Distance eighteen miles.

[Banks] Left camp early. This valley is named Warm Spring Valley. It might be called Hot Spring Valley. There are dozens of springs at the south end pouring forth water which is so hot no man can bear his hand in it. Their volume is such that a creek eight feet wide and two feet deep is supplied by these alone. Nature, as if determined to show her power by strong contrast, has placed a large spring of the coldest water only one hundred and fifty feet from these steaming wonders of the earth. Roads good. Crossed a dividing ridge; now on the headwaters of Mary's River. Our anxiety has been great to reach this spot, to find streams running south seems to afford us great encouragement. This is one great land, or water, mark in our route. Grass good and water (I think) equal to earth's purest fountain. Distance eighteen miles.

The Humboldt to California

August 9—September 20

[Exactly four months after taking leave of St. Joseph the Buckeye Rovers started from the headwaters of the Humboldt on the final five hundred miles to the gold regions. All suffering and hardship to that point were dwarfed by comparison to the grueling trek across burning desert and precipitous mountains as the Ohioans pierced the final barrier blocking the path to California.]

AUGUST 9: [Armstrong] *We left camp about sunrise. Two miles to a canyon where we go through it. A going through we cross the stream nine times in eight miles. It is a very bad road. There is a road that leads to the left. It strikes a small stream before it strikes the main stream. It comes in to the other road in about twenty miles. The creek is small here. Distance eighteen miles.*

[*Banks*] Left camp at sunrise. All anxious to be first in getting through a canyon just ahead. Two wagons in advance of us. We crossed this branch nine times in what is termed eight miles; I think not more than five miles. It is a difficult and dangerous pass between two mountains. The road is rocky and the stream miry. It possesses one grand object; a warm spring of the most transparent clearness, gushing from the mountainside. Nothing can surpass it in beauty. The road the balance of this day good, grass good. Encamped on the same stream. Distance eighteen miles.

AUGUST 10 [Armstrong] *We left camp very early. The teams travel very fast this morning. The roads are good. We crossed the main stream today. It is small. It is nineteen miles from the west end of the canyon. Its grass and water good. The dust is very bad; the drivers have to suffer now. Distance twenty miles.*

[Banks] If good roads, fine grass and water, accompanied with excellent health can cause satisfaction to men placed in our situation, then we should be satisfied. I have never seen meadows to exceed these in luxuriousness. The beautiful red clover adds its grandeur. Those who came by Salt Lake say that the celebration of the 24th of the July by the Mormons was a grand affair. All were invited, not less than five thousand dined, speeches were made, and all passed off glibly. This is the day on which they arrived after a weary pilgrimage in the valley of the Salt Lake. They are represented as cheerful and happy, possessing an abundance of the necessities of life. The climate salubrious. Here we have hard frost some nights. The accounts of suffering behind us, which I heard today, would be incredible to any person except one who has passed this season. The tale of woe will chill many hearts. Encamped on Mary's River. Winds very violent. Whirlwinds of matchless grandeur are daily witnessed. I have heard of but never seen anything to compare with this; the dust mounts in a majestic column to the skies, the woe to a poor fellow's eyes, his lungs, and face. Weather fine. Distance eighteen miles.

AUGUST 11: [Armstrong] *We are camped on the river. Good water and the best grass we have had since we left the States. Distance eighteen miles.*

[Banks] The rush now seems tremendous, each

determined to head his neighbor. Cattle generally are in good condition. Nearly all have stopped to recruit and are anxious to recover lost time. Roads now like ashes, from six to twelve inches deep. Indians beginning to commit depredations. Saw a horse they had shot with an arrow through his left hind leg. The Digger Indians are poor degraded race and they steal through necessity rather than choice. I learn many of the emigrants intend wintering at Salt Lake. We passed two canyons of the river. Distance sixteen miles.

AUGUST 12: [Armstrong] *Sunday. We only drove three miles. We want to rest our cattle. The grass is good and water the same. Distance three miles.*

[*Banks*] Moved a little down the river for better grass. Washed today. Can wash pretty well; it must pass that is certain. Have not shaved these three months, look like a Dunkard. Not one half shave. Some six Indians caught three horses (one of which they shot and scared all) for some men. They were given some ten dollars worth of clothing and food. They stayed with the men last night. They were given blankets to sleep on. They decamped in the night taking the blankets, and a little farther back wounded five or six oxen expecting they would be left. Last night I was on watch and kept my gun near me determined to use it if necessary. Our cattle nearly as dear as life because without them our chance is poor. Encamped on good grass, which is confined to the river bottom. The rest is almost chalky white, destitute of vegetation, except a small greasewood shrub and gloomy sage. A barren waste. Distance two miles.

AUGUST 13: [Armstrong] *Monday morning. We leave camp very early. We laid by to recruit our cattle yesterday. We passed Dr. C. Howell's company from Arkansas. The company lost* eleven head of cattle last night by the Indians. They had ten or twelve men a hunting them. I have seen the Doctor since; they only found two head. One of them they found coming back and the other the Indians had at their camp, cripple so they could not start him. Distance seventeen miles.

[*Banks*] An Arkansas company lost eleven head of cattle last night; supposed to be the work of Indians. Their trail was discovered half a mile below the camp going up into the mountains on the opposite side of the river. They judged by the signs three Indians were driving them. The men are fully bent on revenge. All the emigrants are excited. One proposes shooting every Indian seen on the road.[1] I said it was a dangerous doctrine; very few inclined to his opinion. Some of our men saw two Indians in a state of nudity secreted in the willows. As soon as discovered they ran as if they were in a great hurry; nothing afterwards seen of them. One of the oxen was found eight or ten miles below with a train. When stopped by the men they said it was in great fury. They could scarcely stop him. The Indians, I suppose, caused a stampede to get them beyond the camp. We intend for the future to have our arms with us when we watch the cattle. Encamped opposite Martin's Fork, which we can see comes through a deep chasm in the mountains. Grass poor. Had to cross the river for wood. Distance seventeen.

AUGUST 14: [Armstrong] *This morning we traveled through a canyon which was about six miles through. We crossed the river four times. The river which we forded was gravelly bottom. The grass rather poor where we nooned. I saw an advertisement for four stolen horses; two hundred dollars reward for horses and thief. We crossed Martin's Fork, a little stream that empties into Mary's River. Here we have to cross over* hills. We leave the river for twenty miles. We don't start across till morning. Distance eighteen miles.

[Banks] This morning we came through a canyon. Crossed the river four times in perhaps as many miles. Traveling not very bad. Saw a notice offering two hundred dollars reward for five horses and the thieves that stold them. Some of the horses they have recovered. Many are packing through on their backs, afraid to remain with their teams for fear of freezing to death in the mountains. Six passed this day. They carry but little provisions and generally go on the spunging order. A hard experiment, as the emigrants, with few exceptions, have thrown away everything thought not necessary to their own safety. The face of the country is much changed. It appears white and sterile. Distance eighteen miles.

AUGUST 15: [Armstrong] We started before daylight this morning. Just before we got up the watch discovered something in the shape of a man. They spoke to him and he ran. They supposed he was an Indian after the cattle. The Indians have commenced stealing and shooting the cattle with the bows and arrows. They crippled several. The tramp over the hill was rather dry. We found no water till we got ten miles; there we found two or three little springs, but they were not sufficient to water stock. We drove to the river for feed and water. When we got there we found that there was no grass. I saw a man that had been there for some days. He had lost a horse, and there had been forty head of cattle stolen, and several other horses. There was a party out after the cattle and Indians. While we were lying there the men came in. They killed three out of four Indians. They found some of the meat a drying. The whites came on them. One man by the name of Captain King, from Dayton, Ohio, got shot three or four times, but he killed the Indian and took his bow and arrows.[2] Another by the same name killed one. I seen the bow he took from him. He used to live in London, Ohio. We are distance, twenty-two miles.

[*Banks*] Had a dry stretch of twenty miles to cross; barren and disagreeable, a little water in small springs, but not enough for cattle. Started before daylight. When we reached the river no grass, but all was excitement. The Indians have aroused a storm that may fall heavily on them. They stole eleven head of cattle here last night. One man who has a wife and seven children robbed of horses; his situation is deplorable. This caused some twenty men to go well armed in pursuit of the Indians. Four of the party saw the same number of Indians; killed two and wounded one. The main body saw some one hundred fifty savages, but thought best to retreat. I talked with one of the men that killed an Indian. At the request of some of them I wrote a notice advising emigrants to unite in larger companies (for most of the companies are divided, some going alone). The Indians have signal fires. All are prepared. Traveled till after dark. Scarcely any grass. Left two oxen too poor. Distance twenty-three miles.

AUGUST 16: [Armstrong] *We leave camp early on account of the grass being poor. We camped with the Franklin County, Missouri, company. They had two horses stolen last night and cannot find them. The grass is poor for fifteen miles. The trains are very thick on this river. We crossed the river once today. Distance sixteen miles.*

[*Banks*] Roads very deep dust constantly agitated by wind. No grass for us. The first emigrants had a little.

More cattle and horses missing. No Indians seen on the road. Whites not much better; most of the horses, it is thought, are taken by emigrants. Yesterday a light shower. Distance fifteen miles.

AUGUST 17: [Armstrong] *Left camp at sunrise. We drove till nine a.m. and laid there till noon. The grass was good one mile from the road. There was a very heavy wind and great appearance of rain, but there was none. Good grass where we are camped tonight. Distance fourteen miles.*

[*Banks*] Left camp at sunrise. Our oxen look bad. About nine a.m. we found excellent grass a mile and one-half from the road, and rested until afternoon. Last night a man died leaving a wife and three children; also a woman leaving a husband and family, three young. This expedition is fruitful of calamity. The only tree for many miles is willow. It might be weeping willow. We see many of the gaudy sunflower, and some mint; no others remind of home. Encamped on good grass. Distance fourteen.

AUGUST 18: [Armstrong] *Left camp a little after sunrise. The night cold and windy. It seems immaterial where a man sleeps so he is warm. No rain and scarcely any dew to wet a person. We are near where the Indians are committing some depredations almost every night, but they have not molested our train. The Root Diggers and Shoshones are the devils that bother here. They are destitute of any kind of clothing. The Shoshones are uncommonly large and haired over like dumb brutes. I heard yesterday that the Sioux are a stealing from the emigrants. The Regulars and the Sioux have had a fight; it was a hard fight but the Regulars came out best. The supposition is that the Indians will murder a great many and the last emigrant. Distance sixteen miles.*

[*Banks*] Left camp a little after sunrise. The air fresh and bracing, the atmosphere almost as dry as the earth. It seems immaterial where one sleeps so he is warm. Mr. Gardner sick; too old for such fatigue, fifty-six. Report says the Sioux are stealing all they can; that they fought the troops bravely but were repulsed. Also that many of the emigrants have returned in consequence. Here the report is a fresh company are going in pursuit of the Diggers. Grass good. Distance sixteen.

AUGUST 19: [Armstrong] *We keep down the river till noon. The guide book says we took [words illegible] before we leave the river. We leave it for nine miles. The river runs the crookedest of any river I ever seen; short bends and pretty deep in places. Distance sixteen miles.*

[*Banks*] As I was watching this morning, my eyes heavy with sleep, I thought of the strangeness of human life; how anxious we are for periods of time to pass, yet how we dread the final catastrophe. I little wonder that shepherds should be the founders of astronomy. As one lays on the earth he feels his loneliness and seeks companions in those beautiful forms that seem to speak to him from the sky. (In this atmosphere they shine with uncommon brillancy.) How I have watched star after star as it lifted its shining face above the horizon. The stars of which Job sung were looking on me as they looked on him. O how many millions who mingle in mother earth might say the same could they speak from the dust! But wonder shines the queen of the morning, the harbinger of the king of day; beauty's bright form of hope. Welcome, welcome day. Nothing unusual this day. Distance sixteen miles.

AUGUST 20: [Armstrong] *We drove off the road about one*

mile to get grass and water. The road went around a canyon. There was a road went down the river which was the nearest and best track, but we did not know it before we started. It was about six miles over the hill and three down stream. We camped where there is quite a large island. Distance twenty miles.

[Banks] Left an ox. Country very sterile. No wonder this river sinks; more wonder it runs. The earth like a dry sponge sucking it, and no supply from springs or streams. Its banks contract, its current only tells you are not seeking its source. This is Mary's River, one of the wonders of this wonderous land. Today I stopped behind to fish where Indians has been threshing sunflowers. When I sought the camp I had a difficult job. I thought perhaps they were behind and I retraced my steps two and a half miles, only to learn they were three miles ahead. I walked very fast eight miles, and in the dark, solitary, and alone across a ridge when I came to the river. I missed them and stopped with an Arkansas train. They came only seventeen miles. I had walked twenty-three miles. (I had no coat with me.)

AUGUST 21: [Armstrong] The trains are beginning to push. Provisions are getting rather scarce. The emigrants threw away so much back on the Platte, and till within a few days back, meat from fifteen to twenty cents per pound, sugar fifty cents, flour from ten to twenty dollars. The alkali is bad. The ground has a kind of scale which is quite hard. The land looks like ashes. It has a very disagreeable smell. It injures the grass. Distance sixteen miles.

[Banks] I rested on the roadside as I believed they were behind. A little before ten I saw them; it seemed like a reunion of old friends. Where I stopped last night there were four others in a like *fix*. All seem in great hurry. Oxen failing. Grass very poor, some this noon middling. Distance sixteen miles.

AUGUST 22: [Armstrong] *We leave camp early this morning. We swam the cattle over the river. We are about trading wagons today with a man from Illinois. He belongs to the Union Band, and W. S. Wilson is going to drive the man's team a while for his board. We leave tonight. We get a lighter wagon and one we think will answer our purpose as well as the ones we have got, and be two hundred lighter. Distance eighteen miles.*

[*Banks*] The roads are deep sand, worse than before Sunday. [August 19] One living in a fertile land can form no correct idea of this feral, dreary waste. To travel month after month without seeing anything worthy of the name of tree, and the moment you leave a stream, no grass, even here you seldom see good grass. The ground must be low. Today passed thousands of acres of swamp, bullrushes, some ten feet high. The upland, if of a sandy or loamy nature, sinks beneath one's feet, being burrowed in all directions by squirrels, moles, and prairie dogs. Our provisions present a hungry prospect. William Wilson has engaged to drive for an Illinois man through for his board. Five months and not through, a long tedious journey. Distance sixteen miles.

AUGUST 23: [Armstrong] *It looks very much like rain this morning, but I don't think we will get any, for it is very uncommon through these parts. I have not seen any rain for several weeks, and but little then. The ground is as dry as ashes. The roads are very heavy and sandy. The sand is from three to six inches deep. We crossed the river again to the south side. Distance fifteen miles.*

[*Banks*] Deep sand worse than yesterday. Some of the men talk of packing the rest of the distance, some two hundred fifty miles. Stormy and very much like rain. Some thunder. Dust like fog. All well. Distance fourteen miles.

AUGUST 24: [Armstrong] *Friday. Two of our men started to pack through on their backs. They only took provisions to last them through, which is considered ten days' travel. Steadman and Ferris of Michigan. We crossed the creek several times today. Distance fifteen miles.*

[*Banks*] Two started to pack, Steadman and Ferris. They expect to go over thirty miles a day. Bad roads keep us company. It is most wonderful how these bodies of sand were ever brought together; hills of sand, and plains of sand. Grass scarce, oxen look bad. Distance fifteen miles.

AUGUST 25: [Armstrong] *More of our men got in the notion of packing, Asa Condee and W. H. Smith of Wisconsin who belong to our train. Last night we camped near some Mormons that was returning to Salt Lake. They have been to the gold mines. They gave us some encouragement about the gold. They inform us that there is a road some twelve miles from here that takes to the right hand; it strikes the gold regions in the distance of one hundred forty-six miles.[3] It is sixty miles without wood, grass, or water, and a great many dead cattle. Men that go it cut grass to last sixty miles. We passed the road today about two o'clock. Between seven and eight hundred wagons gone it. Distance eighteen miles.*

[*Banks*] We hear of a cutoff leading to Feather River, a distance of one hundred forty-six miles. There gold is said to be plenty. Many wagons gone, some seven hundred. Hedgepath first opened it.[4] No grass for the first sixty miles, a very serious difficulty. Condee and Smith gone ahead packing. Our numbers materially decreasing. Saw the road to the right, determined not to take it. A host of notes left here for friends; lines on cards and boards, all open for general inspection. Matter? Why, taking this or that road, state of health, condition of cattle, and company. Some of them well written; others, the schoolmaster certainly was abroad. To many that going this journey will prove a curse; health or disease, wealth or poverty. The mind, that which distinguished man from the beast, will be depraved. A vast number are underage, some mere boys, cursing and swearing, carrying knives and pistols; men, and that savage men, in their own estimation. Some are going miles for grass to take on the cutoff, a poor prospect. Everything appears rather dreary. "Never give up." Bought one hundred pounds bacon, fifteen dollars. Traveled late in search of food for our cattle. Poor. Distance seventeen miles.

Would have lain bye today had we found grass. This country is arid, dreary and wretched. Its very ugliness makes it a curiosity. The plains on this river seem to be under water half the year. It appears like the bottom of a pond baked smooth and cracked; the least touch and it becomes dusty. This day we passed over seven miles of a sage bed (fourteen miles of the same above we partly avoided). The sage six to twelve inches high and miserably poor. It is astonishing ought could live in such a place, yet there are a few hares (these must visit the river occasionally). I saw three or four lizzards, one or two flies; one must pity them. Here are thousands of small lumps of black grass, no doubt formed by the union of alkali and sand in some of the many fires of this region. We found some berries on the river bank, in appearance like red currents, taste like a lemon. We had not of any such on this route and rather fearful after eating them. Now as I write a grand whirlwind is passing over. The sight is sublimely grand, a vast column of dust towering toward the sky. The berries we found are named buffalo berries, for what reason I know not. The bush is the largest timber for some hundreds of miles. William Wilson takes the road to Feather River so we may not see him in some months. I asked him what I should tell Amanda if I should see her before him. "Take care of Charlie." E. Ferrill thought he would try the same road packing on an ox picked up lame. Started in the morning; in the evening we seen him driving his ox into camp. We had some fun. Traveled till dark. Found a little grass. Here the river runs through a deep chasm. Distance seventeen miles.

AUGUST 27: [Armstrong] *We have been on a dry streak, we might say for two days. Teams do drive off the road to water but there is only two places where the road comes to the river. Distance seventeen miles.*

[*Banks*] The aspect of the country unchanged. Every step seems to bring greater sterility to view. Could not get nearer than one half mile of the river. Its banks are too steep and rough; we are one hundred feet above the stream. The air feels like fall. We cannot judge here by the foliage; it looks pretty well crisped nearly all seasons. Distance fourteen miles.

AUGUST 28: [Armstrong] *Shortly after we had started we seen a man just from the mines. He belonged to Walker's train from Missouri. He sent this man on to see what prospects there was. He has twenty men hired. This man reports favorably. He says any man is sure a ten dollars per day. He says a man can make one ounce per day without much difficulty. He thinks we can get there in three weeks. It is very dusty today, the wind blows very hard. It is twenty miles to* water from here. No grass. We drive through without grass or water. Distance twenty-three miles.

[*Banks*] Hear there is luxurious grass within reach of this day's trail. Saw a man returning from California to meet his company. Provisions cheap, gold plenty, roads middling good. Going by Feather River not advisable; altogether news highly encouraging. We are now encamped on Mary's River twenty miles above the Sink. Our journey this day was like the few days past; until night we saw nothing encouraging, but heard there was ten thousand acres of good grass four miles farther. We found it and so did our cattle, to their no small delight. Left one more ox this day. This vast meadow is a marsh, but not deep enough at this season to mire cattle. We cannot easily reach the river. We use that [water] from holes three or four feet deep, rather poor. Intend to remain one or two days to recruit. Distance twenty miles.

AUGUST 29: [Armstrong] *Last evening we drove across the first slough of the Sink. We did not get grass till nine o'clock at night. We have understood there is good grass two miles below here. We start for there this morning. We have to cut grass to last for sixty miles. Here we expect to lay here two days. There is a great many teams here a recruiting. Here grass is very good. Distance two miles.*

[*Banks*] Moved two miles lower down, grass better. Cut grass to make hay to take for our teams. From this grass to Truckee River, some seventy miles, there is no grass and but little water. All are taking it. Many Indians visited us. They are the most intelligent and the best clad we have seen. Some have been in California diggings, hence their superiority. Some speak a few words of English. One old man described our journey, drew a map of the gold region, San

Francisco, and company, described a ship and steamboat, was very communicative. Said their squaws were now in the diggings. They call themselves Piutes.[5] Weather as cold as October in Ohio. Nights very cold and frosty, middle of the day pleasant. Here the river spreads out in wide marshes, yet has a channel. Twenty miles below it ends its race. All well.

AUGUST 30: [Armstrong] *We are still a laying here, yet teams are continually coming in here. Not a great number started out yet. There is plenty of Indians here. They call themselves Piutes. They live in the Sierra Nevada Mountains. Several of them has been to the mines. They can give a pretty fair description of the road.*

[*Banks*] Mended my boots this day. Those who came last night or this morning busy cutting grass. Some carrying on their backs, others on horses, some take wagons. A wagon without a cover a strange sight to us, the whole affair a novelty. The Indians appear willing to work. They have been busy carrying wood; a little food all the pay they get. Water is better than I thought. Remained in camp.

AUGUST 31: [Armstrong] *This morning we leave this place. We are twenty-five miles above the Sink of the Mary's River. The road for ten miles or more is just like an ash bed. The oxen sink into it from four to twelve inches. We have had no grass for the cattle at noon. We got to the Sulphur Springs about sunset. We laid there till eleven o'clock and we started. We have fifty miles without grass or water, and we have to drive day and night till we get there. We have drove all night and till three or four o'clock in the afternoon. We laid here till about sunset and it is one of the greatest sights that I ever seen of the kind. There was from twenty to thirty springs; the water had to be cooled for to drink and after it was par-*

tially cool it was not fit to drink. It did not get cool, that is perfectly cool, in sixteen hours. There was some that boiled up out of the spring from six to eighteen inches. I seen some pieces of meat a boiling in it. There had been about twenty wagons left and burnt up there. The road today has fairly filled up with cattle that has given out. Distance from Sulphur Springs to the Hot Springs is twenty-five and it is called twenty-five to Truckee River, the nearest water. We traveled all night. About sunrise we reached the sand hill nine miles from the river. We had nine of our oxen to give out, and we have to leave one wagon here and put all of the oxen to one wagon to get it to the river. We got to the river about ten o'clock. We stayed there till next morning. Two of us started back to the other wagon. I never seen such a destruction of property in my life. We seen about forty wagons, and something near one hundred fifty head of dead cattle and given out altogether, and more than one hundred log chains, ox yokes, etc. The night we got the last wagon in we drove about two miles up the river. It is said we cross this stream twenty-seven times in twenty-eight miles. Distance fifteen.

[*Banks*] Left camp before sunrise. We have a hard drive before we rest. The earth here is a species of peat; it is formed principally by the roots of prairie cane. It is two feet deep. Hundreds of acres are burnt and fires are yet burning, in many places leaving vast quantities of light ashes to be agitated by every breeze. We nooned near the Sink (at least where it is at this season). It spreads out in marshes and shallow lakes. Here the water is saline. At dusk we reached what is properly the Sink. An embankment some twenty feet high extends across the bed of the river, extending from mountain to mountain, perhaps one and a half miles wide. Mountaineers say that in the spring when the snow is melting the river forms a large lake many miles long, which is confirmed by its present appearance, being completely level and destitute of vegetation. The barrier has all the regularity of art, and what is remarkably strange, it has a large slough on the opposite side in the corner next the river. No water but from wells which are impregnated with sulphur. The slough is miry. We rest here two or three hours then push on. Distance twenty-five miles.

SEPTEMBER 1: [Banks] Commenced traveling at eleven p.m. This the first day of fall. As I watched the sun rise over the mountain top I was thinking of human life; how wonderful it changes and how brief its span. Season after season rolls along, we heed them not, except occasionally to give them a passing thought as milestones in the journey of life. If we have an object in view, we count the distance, we measure *time*, ernestly looking to the end we push on, scarcely dreaming this is the journey of life. This region is awfully volcanic in all its outlines; blackness, barrenness, and lava. We came to Boiling Springs at noon.[6] The child calls the last toy the prettiest. An admirer of nature may be pardoned if he calls the last wonder the mightiest. What can be more amazing than to see boiling water bursting in all directions from the side of a hill. They are generally small, but one contains hundreds of barrels of water. One small one near foams and rages like a boiling pot. I saw meat cooked in one, it was completely done. The water is cooled for cattle in pools, or as best you can. All are busy cooling. The water produces strangury and is very disagreeable. We leave here at dusk. Cattle generally look very bad. Distance twenty-five.

SEPTEMBER 2: [Banks] Some think they see the elephant.[7] If fatigue, weariness, constant excitement, and awful distress among cattle make the sight, he is surely here. We scarcely made a halt until today at noon we reached Salmon Trout River.[8] To us it seems not less than twenty-five miles. This day we scarcely were out of the smell of putridity. Not less than two hundred carcasses of oxen and horses are strewn along the road within thirty miles. Some moping about waiting for death, no possibility of other relief. Upwards of fifty log chains stretch along like lengthy serpents, their owners having no further use for them. Seven of our cattle failed; some we expect to get in. We had to doubleteam and go back eight miles for the other wagon. The stream is large, clear, and beautiful. Grass poor. It is wonderful to see cattle rush in the water. They drink, they stand, now taste it. O how delicious! I know it was to me. Fifty hours and not more than three of them in sleep.

SEPTEMBER 3: [*Banks*] I have been herding all day, grass middling. As I was picking up pieces of books and newspapers (a great many destroyed, even maps), I was surprised to see the name of Mr. Edmonds, Keeper of the Tombs. So much for being a public character. I rather suspect he would rather his name were here than himself. Got in our wagon and all our cattle. One we will leave on account of weakness. It is a wonderful and painful sight to see teams coming in from the desert. Some wagons left and others have gone out for them. We hear five hundred wagons are at the Sink. I fear the desert will prove a sink to many of them. I saw a fine looking Missourian who was in the habit of swearing; an overdose has cured him. The profanity of this road should disgust any person of spirit. Crossed the river one time. We start again in the morning.

SEPTEMBER 4: [Armstrong] *We are anxious to get through.*

Only eighty miles to the summit of the Sierra Nevada Moun-
tains. We drove but a short distance. This is one of the long-
est canyons we have come across yet. We crossed the river
two times. It is the swiftest stream that I ever seen, and the
rockiest one. Distance six miles.

[*Banks*] We must travel many miles in a can-
yon of this roaring torrent. No grass. A rough, stony road.
Crossed the river twice. The aspect of things wild in the extreme, weather delightful. The scenery is relieved by the gay
foliage of cottonwood trees. They are large and fine looking,
and certainly a novelty, the first in five hundred miles. Distance six miles.

SEPTEMBER 5: [Armstrong] *The roads part of the time very*
stony and part very good. Crossed nine times. Distance ten
miles.

[*Banks*] We of course have no difficulty in
finding the road. It is as plain as Broadway, but how the first
who traveled this route ever discovered a possibility of bringing wagons, to an eye witness is truly astonishing.[9] The road
rough, the crossing of the river frequent, the bottom rocky,
and current almost impossible to stand. In fording this evening some of our men were nearly swept away. The river is so
clear you see the stony bottom at any depth. We are in sight
of the Sierra Nevada Mountains. Crossed Truckee River nine
times. Grass good. Distance ten miles.

SEPTEMBER 6: [Armstrong] *We still keep winding up to-*
ward the mountains. The farther we get up the swifter it is.
It is almost out of the question for a man to wade it without
having something to support him. Several of our men have
been taken down in wading. I have had to hold on to the ox
bow to support myself. We are encamped on as good grass as

I most ever seen. The valley is from five to six miles wide and about six long; that is the wide part of it. After we left the wide part of the valley we go over a hill. It is very stony. We struck the river in about four miles after we left the valley. Where we struck the river we came to some pine timber, the first one was the largest pine trees that I ever seen. It was five feet over. We nooned there. We drove about two miles farther. We crossed the river once. Distance fifteen.

[*Banks*] Much the same as yesterday; roads wonderfully bad. Crossed the river ten times. In the evening as we climbed a hill, a beautiful prospect opened to our view; thousands of acres of green meadow encircled by lofty mountains. The contrast was wonderful; on one side all fertility, on the other all sterility. Wherever the river inundates the bottoms in a high stage of water we find grass. This is generally the case. The number of encampments here reminds me of Platte. Came late but our journey was not very long. Fifteen miles.

SEPTEMBER 7: [Armstrong] *Early this morning we started. It was on some distance before the teams and I discovered some of our boys at one side of the road very busily engaged. I went out and found they were digging onions. There was no appearance of any green tops; how they were discovered I do not know. They were fine eating. Distance twelve miles.*

[*Banks*] Most of this day the roads were well macadamized, except the stones were rather large, being often the size of a bushel, and from that to a peck. We found a large bed of onions, the first vegetables of the season. Crossed river twice. Distance twelve miles.

SEPTEMBER 8: [Armstrong] *Early this morning we were aroused by the guards. They came in and told us that one of* our oxen shot with an arrow and one missing. The guard went to sleep and did not wake until nearly daylight. The one they had drove off was the best ox we had. He was the largest ox that I have seen on the road. He was quite thin. Eight of us rigged our guns and started in a few minutes. We struck the trail and evidence three hundred yards of the camp. They had killed him and taken the best of the meat and the hide with them. There had been four Indians and drove him out from among the cattle. We found two arrows. They stole two horses and one mule and, I suppose, they packed part of the meat on the horses they stole. After we struck the bluffs we seen Indians' tracks. We went twelve or fifteen miles back into the mountains. We could not see any of them. We seen a great deal of sign. We trailed the fellows to where they had laid down to rest, and there we lost the trail. We did not get in till after dark. We left four men with the team and told them to drive on to good grass. We seen a great deal of sign of the animals but never got sight of them. We wandered around after them. We became discouraged and started for camp. We found our wagons at the last crossing of the twenty-seventh crossing. Distance nine miles.

[Banks] Last evening I thought there was danger of Indians because I saw recent signs, and further the place being in the bend of the river, the mountains near on either side, and no encampment adjacent, would favor their knavish designs. At ten p.m. we saw our cattle were mostly laying down near the camp and bushes all around them. We went to sleep. Before daylight we were collecting them when we saw that one was shot in the left side on the shoulder within an inch or two of his vitals, and that our largest ox was missing, and no doubt stolen as we found blood where he had been driven across the road. Eight of us armed ourselves, determined to give them a chase and worse if we caught them. (They stole two horses and a mule at the same time, and two others belonging to the train that lost the horses went in another direction.) We went some twenty-five miles back in the mountains. We had followed the trail not more than two hundred yards from the road when we saw all they had left of the ox; nearly all his flesh and his skin were carried off. The sight was aggravating. We pushed on. We saw where they slept last night, and many places where they had recently been. We saw a large piece of beef which was dropt, but never saw an Indian. We several times thought we were near them, but they kept out of sight. We saw some curiosities. A small salt lake having two or three inches of beautiful white crust as pure as snow in appearance. The pines are large and majestic, often four and five feet in diameter. The country is wild and rugged, but not devoid of sublime scenery. Three of us came to the river near sundown, and crossed on an Indian bridge displaying much ingenuity. Some of their baskets made of willow are neat looking, but they are a villainous set. They have stolen more than one hundred head of cattle and many horses, leaving some in a deplorable situation. Six of us came in this evening. In the meantime our team came nine miles.

SEPTEMBER 9: [Armstrong] *Sunday morning. We leave Truckee for several miles. We now come where there is plenty of timber. It is pine trees and nothing else. We drove over a mountain to a small valley where there had been plenty of grass and water. The grass is almost eaten off. Distance six miles.*

[Banks] All are in that were engaged in that foolish game yesterday. Lots of fellows are now engaged in firing at a mark, no better than a regular army. Something which has proven very disagreeable to many of us I must mention. Graham and Reeves brought two oxen from the desert; finding no claimant, we brought them on and worked them. A Missouri company with which we were acquainted it appears owns them. They say they drove them in the team across the river and that we stole them. This is generally believed to our no small annoyance. There is certainly a mistake somewhere. One cannot be too much on his guard. I am sorry we ever had an connection with the oxen, but I may here add it has been generally understood whatever property left, oxen or otherwise, ceased to be claimed by their former owner. Enough of this. Our journey today has been in the mountains, through a grand forest of large and lofty pines, the largest I have ever seen. We are now twenty-six miles from the summit of the Sierra Nevada Mountains, making slow progress. Encamped in a valley where once was good grass, now but little. It is strange but true: wherever you find grass it must be prairie, even in the mountains. Elsewhere there is no timber (as I elsewhere mentioned) except on streams. All well. Distance eight miles.

SEPTEMBER 10: [Armstrong] *We have concluded to stay here and rest our cattle. When we got here yesterday they were in high glee a shooting, and today it is pretty much the same thing.*

[Banks] Remained in camp to recruit our cattle as we hear the prospect is not flattering ahead. I have been reading a part of a magazine I think belongs to the Dublin University Magazine. Its leading articles are strongly Orange and decidedly Tory, abusing O'Connell, praising Wellington. Its date, April, 1843. How pleasing even this seemed to one cut off from the rest of the world, as a sweet morsel to a hungry man. To trace its history would be amusing, but I opine difficult. We found a fishing pole (elegantly made) stamped "Bell Alley Temple Bar." It was hid in a clump of willows.

SEPTEMBER 11: [Armstrong] *This morning we start out for the mountains again. This is the best pine timber I ever seen. At noon we struck a small creek which is called twelve miles from where we left this morning. We drove six miles farther in the afternoon. We are camped in a small valley. Distance eighteen miles.*

[*Banks*] We were wakened in the night by the howling of wolves. Their serenade is horrible, yet they inflict it on us almost every night. Sometimes I have listened with a kind of pleasure as their shrill voices seemed to cleave the air. Such as it is, we must put up with it. We are in the mountains and the roads are better than since we came on the Truckee. We are again deceived on the pleasing side. Grass good. Encamped in a pleasant little valley, well watered. Distance fourteen miles.

SEPTEMBER 12: [Armstrong] *This morning as one of the trains were driving out their cattle to graze just before the dawn of day, they came on two Indians that was watching a chance to steal horses or oxen. They followed them over the hill and shot at them and missed them. Distance thirteen miles.*

[*Banks*] Last night on watch, on my feet constantly from twelve to daylight. The night very cold. We thought we heard Indians piping like young turkeys. As a man was going with cattle a little below us about daybreak he saw two Indians jump from behind a low bank not more than two hundred yards from us. We had built a fire on mountainside that shone over the ground occupied by our cattle. This, and being on the alert, foiled the poor naked gentlemen. If they had not a cool job I am mistaken. The country abounds with game. Much as I deplore their situation, I must feel indignant at such villainy. This evening we saw the cabins (a part of them, some being destroyed) built by the unfortunate Donner and companions.[10] They cut the logs when the snow was six feet deep, as the height of the stumps attest. The account of their sufferings, as given by Bryant, appears horribly corroborated by the piles of broken bones. To me it appeared equalled only by some awful shipwreck. Now the serpent and lizzard occupy the former home of sorrow. We are now within seventeen miles of the mountain. Grass rather poor. Some of us feasted on gooseberries; they are small, and in color purple, somewhat acid in taste. Here we leave the headwaters of the Truckee. It falls seven hundred feet in ninety miles. We have crossed it in all twenty-seven times. The Indians give us some trouble and some fun. We fired three salutes for their benefit, we were answered by other camps, which made the forest ring. Encamped in a bottom almost covered with brush. We tied up our cattle. Distance thirteen miles.

SEPTEMBER 13: [Armstrong] *Yesterday we passed some cabins where Donner and his party suffered. It is at Truckee Lake. The lake is about eight miles from the summit. We camped one mile from the foot of the mountain. It was quite hard work to get up; we had eight yoke of cattle to the wagon. We did not go all the way up the old road, but a short distance we went a little to the right of the old road. They had to haul the wagon up with a windlass. We got up* and down on to the valley of Yuba Valley. It was very rough. We thought we had got over the worst then, but a man by the name of Childs, he was from the mines, he had been a soldier for four years, he said the elephant was before us. Distance nine miles.

[*Banks*] The appearance of the mountain is not as grand as I anticipated. The quantity of snow is small in comparison with the Wind River Mountains. The first of the ascent is gradual but rocky. Within three hundred feet of the summit there is considerable piece of bottom land well watered. The whole mountain is covered by a noble forest of pine. From this point the road is desperate, perhaps an angle of forty-five degrees, strong and sliding. By double-teaming and hard work we reached the summit without accident. Here we dined; our fare was low but our position lofty, being more than nine thousand feet above the sea. The prospect is limited by mountains on either side. The whole country is a series of lofty mountains and deep chasms, with small bottoms. Encamped in valley, grass and water good. Distance ten miles.

SEPTEMBER 14: [Armstrong] We leave the valley this morning and we begin to find the roads as we was informed. We have reached the Devil's Peak. There is some grass and the worst roads that I ever seen. We leave here this morning for the peak. The roads commence to get bad; several places where the wagons has to be let down with ropes. The stones was as thick as they could lay on the road. The wagons are now over rocks the wheels would fall two feet off of. We have seen small lakes all day. It is the head of Bear River. We struck the river just at night. There was an old grave there. We camped here. About twelve o'clock at night the guard gave the alarm of Indians. We all got up and prepared for them. Just before we got up there was two horses came running apast our camp. We caught one of them. Just at daylight another one came up.

[*Banks*] The stream on which we encamp is called Yuba. A Mr. Childs of Kearny's dragoons staid with us last night. He is on his homeward trip after an absence of five years, having seen much hardship, which his many wounds attest. Nine months' labor in the mines gave him knowledge which to us was very important. Simply this; not quite as flattering as we had heard. Those cabins spoken of above are commonly called "Cannibal Cabins." Kearny's troops burnt human bones and human skeletons; the bones were sawed in small pieces to get the marrow. The appearance of the place was very revolting to my eyes. Roads stony and bad. Encamped under Devil's Peak, a lofty and very remarkable mountain. Grass middling. Nearly all the grass for many miles is on small plains which were formerly lakes, and even now they are generally marshy. The aspect of the country wild in the extreme. Rugged, naked rocks on every hand, occasionally relieved by a majestic pine which has seized a foothold. Here the grizzly bear may roam lord for ages. Distance seven.

SEPTEMBER 15: [*Banks*] Saw a small tent near a great rock; no wagon or anything near indicating the owners travelers. Our curiosity was excited. We inquired why they were here. "There is a sick man in the tent and our teams have gone on." Two remained, as I think, to see him die. His countenance had the impress of death. He has been unwell four weeks, yet continued to walk until within two days. A sad sight, but not a strange one on this road. He has no relative near. Encamped without grass. An old grave near enclosed by logs. Distance eight miles.

SEPTEMBER 16: [*Banks*] This [Sunday] almost passed without my knowledge of the day. I could scarcely believe it possible it could pass thus. Such is man a creature of habit. To us there is no day of rest. Yesterday and this day I was so engaged I had not time to write; otherwise this mistake could not occur, and sincerely do I hope it may never again. The sick man whom I mentioned is dead. Superlatives are vain and language weak in an effort to describe the badness of this road; hilly, rocky, sideling, and precipitous. We let the wagons down the rocks some sixty feet in one place; other places we kept the cattle on but attached ropes to ease the wagons down. The ascent was bad enough; stony and difficult, but not precipitous. Some trees we see are truly astonishing, measuring in some instances from five to nine feet in diameter. They are all pines and cedar, their height one hundred fifty to two hundred feet.

Last night about one o'clock two horses came running down the road. At the same time several distinctly heard an ox make the most mournful noises. Indians, we thought, trying to cause a stampede of our cattle. The horses no doubt were scared by them. We were all armed and ready. Some actually saw Indians move; they fired, the object vanished. H. L. Graham went out, swore at one, fired, and came back to the fire feeling wolfish. Presently all was quiet, but we watched till daylight. Now for the awful scene. Two or three trees were badly wounded, but I think they will recover. They were unable to stir, except their tops. They are certainly cripples as far as moving is concerned. Thus ended the farce. The groans came from a dying ox found today; the horses were left loose and wandered off. Our cattle were tied; others near ran loose without guard all night, yet were safe. Encamped on a high mountain, near a clear small lake. Three-fourths of a mile from the road we found excellent grass, which our cattle very much need. Two failed today. We could not bring them to grass. We traveled all day, came not more than six miles.

SEPTEMBER 17: [*Banks*] We ate some gooseberries of a strange appearance, a deep red and as thorny as a stramonium, but somewhat pleasant to taste. The appearance of the soil is that of great fertility. There are wild peas here which very much resemble our garden peas. The sign of bears and deer is plentiful and we had venison for supper last evening. The mountain we came down into this valley is three-fourths of a mile in descent, as steep as any, but not so rocky. Four or five mountains we passed have trees girded by the ropes used in letting down wagons; if a rope breaks the wagon must be dashed to atoms. We have seen more ruins of wagons in the last twenty miles than all together before. Hundreds perhaps are left east of the Sierra Nevada for want of teams. The best picture I could give of these mountains is a vast stairs rising toward the heavens in grand and terrible sublimity, the last almost equalling the first. Such is my opinion of the Sierra Nevadas. Encamped in a valley of a tributary of Bear River, some twenty-five miles from the first diggings. Seventy miles to Johnson's Ranch, which is the first settlement we shall see.[11] This distance we must travel without grass. There was grass, but it has been devoured as if by locusts. We must pull pea vines from the mountainside as the only chance for our cattle. Distance seven miles.

SEPTEMBER 18: [*Banks*] We are getting quite familiar with

Jack Frost; he visits us every night and leaves his card which may be seen late next day. The nights are really cold, and the days not too warm to wear a coat, except when exercising. The sky beautifully clear, and the air always in motion. Water generally pure as ever ran. We remain in camp to recruit our cattle and pull pea vines. Yesterday we left those two which failed. I am glad we left them where there is some chance that they may live. They have been faithful companions of our toil. Of twenty-two head of cattle with which we started, but eleven remain and some of these much reduced. A few look well. Many other companies more unfortunate than we have been.

SEPTEMBER 19: [*Banks*]   Found some pea vines. Traveled slowly. Tried to find gold in some of the streams, had no success. Encamped on very high and picturesque mountain near a noble spring of pure water, near which is a mortar formed in a granite rock, no doubt by the hand of Indians. Distance ten miles.

SEPTEMBER 20: [*Banks*] Learned that there are many digging gold near us with good success. Reached Steep Hollow (a very appropriate name) about four p.m. Fastened trees to our wagons and descended safely. The number of trees at the bottom might remind one of a woodyard.[12] Saw tents which seemed to indicate a permanent residence. Inquired how prospered; some in high spirits, others not so flattering. We are yet one hundred twenty miles from Sutter's fort. The last hill the steepest yet. Encamped on Bear River, a dreary place, but it seems gold is found in small scales nearly all places, especially in the stream. Distance twelve miles.

California
September 21—February 3 *

[The Ohioans reached the periphery of the gold regions at Steep Hollow, on Bear River, after a journey of more than eighteen hundred miles. In spite of hardship and privation they had suffered no losses in lives and had retained essentially the same organization since leaving Ohio more than five months earlier. After prospecting briefly along the Bear and the northern branch of the American River, most of the company moved on to find permanent quarters for the approaching winter season.]

SEPTEMBER 21: Some of our men hunting grass, others buying cradles to commence operations. Found no grass. Must drive our cattle to Deer Creek eighteen miles distant.

SEPTEMBER 22: Divided into three companies. I work with Drake and Reeves. Bought a cradle, price ten dollars. Went to work. Worked three hours, made three dollars, some made sixteen dollars or more. Faint heart never won fair lady; one man says he made two or three thousand in as many weeks.

SEPTEMBER 23: Mind very much occupied in thinking of those whom neither time nor place can separate me from. How my heart yearns to see you again. Thought of writing home but will defer till I reach Sutter's. Heard bad news from the States that the cholera raged fearfully; among the victims were Polk and Benton.[1] Felt much pain of mind.

* After September 14, all entries are by Banks.

Uncertainty thou art a canker. Read none this day [Sunday].

SEPTEMBER 30: I know not whether to consider my journey ended or not. Certainly we are in the diggins, but we must go farther. We cannot remain this winter here. Some did however pass last winter near this place. Their cabins remain. The snow was about two feet deep. The floods must have been great. This stream on which we are working was some eleven or fifteen feet above its present level. The whole country seems wild in the extreme. Gold abounds in all its streams, some small quantities also found on the mountain. It is found more plenty in the banks where the current was obstructed by large rocks, and the principal lies in knowing these places. Some turn the stream and realize a handsome reward; others again almost entirely fail. Hence some men are buoyant and contented, others gloomy and dissatisfied. I can't say I belong to this or that class, I feel cheerful enough though not making a fortune. If those succeed, I may, at least hope says so, and I hope she may not be mistaken. Last week we washed over three ounces, worth fifty-seven dollars in all. The cradle and pan are the only instruments used. The cradle is shaped much as its name would indicate; usual length four to five feet, breadth at the bottom twelve inches, the top eighteen, a box placed on top and in the back occupying one third its length. The box contains a screen to prevent large stones or lumps of earth from passing through. Just below this is an apron, or cloth, sloping towards the back of the cradle so that the earth and water must pass through its whole length. The bottom of the cradle is divided by two or three bars to prevent the gold from washing out, which, being much heavier than any of its neighbors, is caught here. The cradle is placed on legs over the stream; the operator seats himself on the left, using his right hand to dash in water while he rocks with the other. The screen is made of zinc, sheet iron, tin, or sticks, the meshes one-fourth to one-half an inch in diameter. With one of these a man will wash from twelve to twenty bushels of earth per day, having one or two men in the meantime to dig and carry it to him. The last washing must be carefully performed in a pan to separate the gold from the black sand which is very heavy and fine. Gold is found from the minutest atom to lumps an ounce or more, the latter very seldom. The cost of the cradle varies with circumstances, some have been as high as $125. Now so many are leaving they are scarcely worth anything. I saw a sheet iron pan holding nearly a peck for which eight dollars had been given. Tin cups, one quart or so, four dollars. As regards edibles, twenty-five cents per pound of flour, fifty cents per pound of pork or bacon, twenty-five per pound of beef are now the prices current in this market. They have been three or four times as high. Bacchus has not many votes here; he sells his potations at fifty cents per dram carefully measured out by his own hand. I have never had much better health in the course of my life than on this journey, and I have not tasted alcohol in any shape whatever since I left Missouri. Here the climate at present is delightful; cool at all times but no frost. We had a few drops of rain last Friday [September 28]; otherwise the sky has been beautifully clear. Many are cor laining of loss of health. This (in my opinion) is caused by indiscretion; laboring too hard and unnecessarily getting their feet and clothes wet. The prevailing disease is diarrhea, which often carries off the patient in three or four weeks. Physician's fee an ounce of gold, no matter how short the distance may be. They are mostly young and inexperienced, and judging by the cognomen "doctor," they are quite numerous. The soil is rich, producing a plentiful growth of timber, principally pine and cedar. There is also some oak. Among smaller productions is one called the soap plant, differing much from that seen on the Platte. It is a bulb enclosed in a thick covering somewhat like very coarse hair. It is white and starchy, rather than soapy, though it will produce a lather. There is no fruit here and nothing to bear it except some miserable grapevines. I have wandered a little from the subject I commenced with. From this time henceforth I must content myself with a weekly notice of such as I may deem worthy of record and this day (Sunday), as I design giving it to rest and meditation, in writing I can profitably employ a part.

OCTOBER 7: How strangely our plans are formed, and how strange the issue. On Monday we went to North Fork with great anticipations. The journey is up the side of a very high mountain and down the opposite into the deepest gorge I had yet seen.[2] Distance nine. Each of us carried a considerable load. We found gold plenty, some of our men washing nine and ten dollars in a few hours. Our cradles were left on Bear River so we determined to carry them over. We walked very fast and being overheated several of us took cold. H. L. Graham was quite sick so that someone must remain with him. I staid expecting in a day or two he would be able to walk over. His disease being dysentery is painful and weakening. My situation was a little irksome. I saw some men from Columbus carry home day after day some twelve to fifteen dollars in coarse gold. I thought our boys were making it faster, but judge my surprise last evening when in two of them came carrying their packs. Could find no place to wash, all the good places occupied. Now for Sacramento city, or some other place. We must seek winter quarters. Off some go for our cattle and I must go and help to pack the balance of our goods from North Fork. This evening the cattle came in. Graham is much better. We will try to climb the mountain out of this hollow tonight.

OCTOBER 14: Two weeks of rest has not increased the strength of our team. Four head are lost, two strayed, and two dead, one a large black and white ox, a favorite with all. He and his mate were a remarkably large, well-shaped, docile, and intelligent yoke. They were badly strained in a marsh this side of South Pass at Willow Springs. We drove them loose five hundred miles. Broad we left at the head of Mary's River. Buck worked faithfully from the time the Indians stole our largest ox until we came to Steep Hollow. One could not look at him and not admire his strength and spirit. Some of our men saw him laying dead where he was mired. The suffering of the brute has been terrible. "The merciful man is merciful to his beast." Three of our company will probably winter in the neighborhood of Deer Creek—Armstrong, Logan, and Barnes.[3] In that place the prospect for dry diggins seem good; for me it is too far north. Today our teams failed and we had no alternative but to leave one of our wagons. When we left St. Joseph we had twenty-two head of cattle and three wagons; now but six oxen and one wagon. This evening I for the first time saw the prairie on fire. To see the fire rushing upward and onward is a beautiful sight. It seems some twenty or thirty miles off. The view of the vast plain formed by the junction of the Feather and Bear Rivers and North Fork with the Sacramento as it bursts on your sight from the mountains is the grandest I have ever beheld. The country since leaving Bear River is the handsomest we have seen for hundreds of miles, but this in a great measure realizes our expectations of California. The government has two companies seven and a half miles west of Johnson's on a fine situation where it intends to erect a fort. We reached Johnson's at eight o'clock. Johnson has been gone two years; some New York men are laying off a town. Encamped three miles below. Distance forty-five from Bear River.

OCTOBER 21: At Sacramento city. I have written home but heard no news from them. I scarcely expected to hear from home, yet I feel disappointed. Thursday evening, shortly after we came on the American on the opposite side from this place, Hugh Dixon hurried over to see his brother or hear from him. He returned with the sad news of the Doctor's death. The Doctor had started to meet us and lost his mule. He then went to work near Sutter's Mill. He little thought of death when the messenger came; as he was prying a rock, the crowbar slipped and knocked his pistol from his breast. As it fell the hammer struck the rock which burst the cap and the bullet passed through his heart. He died without a groan. "In the midst of life we are in death." Of this place and the country adjacent I must say something. This season being the dry part of the year everything appears barren, but there is grass enough for large herds of fat and handsome cattle. They are almost as wild as deer, yet they are nearly all branded and, I suppose, all claimed by some person. Formerly they were of little value, not more than five to eight dollars per head, now probably eighty to a hundred dollars. On the banks of the river there are innumerable quantities of excellent grapes. These to us were a luscious treat. The city is situated one and a half miles below the American on a plot said to have been fifteen feet under water in a remarkable freshet a few years since. Its growth and existence may not be unlike Jonah's gourd; its population is estimated at six thousand, of these fifty may be women and children. Ten of the habitations are tents of cloth stretched on frames; one is made of sheet iron, another of zinc, the balance poor frames. Town lots sell at from eight hundred to seven or eight thousand dollars; ground rent in some instances as high as the best locations in Philadelphia or New York. They were in so much hurry to remove a heavy growth of timber which incumbers the ground, in one instance I saw a large sycamore tree standing in the center of a house. Some are trying to have the place incorporated. At present nascences are neither few nor small. Everything, as might be expected, is on a high scale; flour twenty-two dollars per barrel, pork forty dollars, more or less, potatoes forty cents to sixty per pound, cheese seventy-five cents per pound, tea and coffee low, sugar and molasses moderate. Nearly half the tents (or houses) in town sell liquors. The low doggeries ask twenty-five, the respectable fifty cents per dram. Here we met some of our company who had gone on in advance. They are much debilitated by chill and fever and seem to be deprived of all energy. Wilson we have heard nothing of. This being the grand depot for miners, you see those that come by every route. Many of those who came by the Horn have their fondest hopes blighted by the scurvy. All things considered, their trip was not much better than ours, and in most instances fully as tedious.[4] By the Isthmus, I believe, the shortest, safest, and best route.[5] There is much tragedy and some romance connected with each thoroughfare. Some young men who came by the Horn, when off the coast of Lower California, were told by the Captain they were in the latitude of San Francisco. In their haste to reach the gold, they left the ship in a small boat with two days' provisions. They reached shore but saw nothing but lofty mountains. They walked on the beach and ate mussels. In three weeks, after wonderful privations, they arrived in San Francisco. This evening we leave the city.

OCTOBER 28: I now write at Cold Spring.[6] Five of us came in advance of the team to seek a good location to build, which we find a difficult task. We went first to Sutter's Mill, remained one night. Coloma, a town near it, appears quite neat. Here we saw a bridge which is thrown across South Fork. It is for passengers, toll twenty-five cents. This is the only one I have seen in California. Well, when here a few hours we heard stories showing Cold Spring better by far than this, so off we go. About half a mile west of the town, on a high hill shaped like a mound, we saw the grave of Dr. Dixon. It is the only one which is surrounded with paling. A noble pine waves over the place of death. Its, death's, inmates number twelve.

Here we spent two days prospecting but our success was poor. We see little to encourage, yet others evidently feel otherwise as the town indicates, there being some forty log houses. The location is healthy. On Friday two of us went to Hangtown, or Gallowstown, five miles distant, which place has yielded more gold than any other in California.[7] It is situated on Weaver Creek (so named because Weaver first discovered the diggings).[8] Population three thousand, at least so estimated. The creek is nearly dry perhaps one-half the year. Its bed is dug in deep holes a rod square, four to six feet, or upwards, in depth, which are so near that the earth is banked up with stones to prevent its falling back on them. Many large fortunes have been dug here; in one case several pounds of gold were washed in one pan of dirt, perhaps three or four thousand dollars in one hole. But alas for us, like the snow of last winter, it is nearly all gone. I saw the tree on which three men were hanged. The fatal limb spreads its brawny arm over a house. It is said there is no theft, but the amount of gambling is fearful. We thought best to winter at this place [Cold Spring]. H. Dixon went to meet our team. It came in this morning. Distance forty-five to Sacramento, five to Sutter's Mill.

NOVEMBER 4: Last week we sold our wagon and team for two hundred fifty dollars. Before this we had sold two broken-down oxen for twenty-five dollars. We divided every species of property and each man took his share. So goodbye Buckeye Rovers, you're defunct. We divided on the ground where we intend to build. Three of our former company—Ferrill, Reeves, and Townshend—have gone to crop wood at seven dollars per cord and saw logs at two dollars per log. This sounds strange, but when lumber sells at fifty cents per foot it alters the case. Two men working with a whipsaw make upwards of fifty dollars per day. The timber is good. "When does the wet season commence in California?" was a question often asked. "Generally about Christmas!" the almost universal reply. Writers say in this month; I am afraid this is one of the truths they tell. It commenced to rain on Monday and has continued with but little intermission since. We split clapboards and made a shed, our only protection from the inclemency of the weather. We, however, have all our logs cut and the foundation laid. Our house is to contain two apartments thirteen feet wide. Here we expect to pass six months isolated from (I might almost say) the rest of the world. For my part, if I earn enough to live I shall feel happy. Those whose constitutions can bear it may work in the rain, I can not. At this season the ravines, which have been parched, can be worked. Some of them are very rich. You constantly see men going in all directions with pan, pick, and shovel; some carrying cradles to a place which others are leaving, perhaps to go where the first left. Today we worked some on our house. We are anxious to get in some place of shelter. All are tolerably well.

NOVEMBER 11: Once more in a house. Yes, for six months I have not slept or eaten under a roof. We lived like Arabs, or Tartars, and not much unlike own native sons of the forest. Once more in a house sitting by our own fire. We call it by the name of home. To us it is a home, but how unlike the home of the mind. It rains more or less almost every day. We fear the roads will become almost impassable, if so provisions must rise very much as I fear there is not a sufficient supply in this region. We are waiting, hoping to see more fair weather, perhaps foolishly.

NOVEMBER 18: Weather wet. No prospect of digging at present. Last Tuesday this land of gold, this germ of future greatness, perhaps the place of the last great western nation, saw a wonderful sight—a general election. The adoption of the constitution was the great question. It was not as good as I could wish, yet as good as I expected. It is essentially free.[9] In this region the sentiment is generally in its favor. All who were present were allowed to vote. I voted for it. I would rather the question of freedom or slavery had been boldly met by Congress and settled on the side of right. Of the candidates I knew almost nothing. By report Burnett stood fair, but his address is a miserable affair; voting for him was a leap in the dark into the mire.[10] Provisions rising; flour seventy-five cents and a prospect of being much higher. The roads are very bad; hauling from the city up here fifty to sixty cents per pound. This journey can be performed in six to eight days down and up, four yokes bringing ten to fifteen hogsheads. Employment plenty.

NOVEMBER 25: Weather fine. Some of our men gone four miles to see a canyon in which (some say) hundreds of thousands of dollars of gold were dug. It is a remarkably deep and dangerous looking chasm. At present there is little work done in it, the lateness of the season and the general belief that most of the gold is taken out are the reasons. I felt too unwell to accompany them, being troubled with the dysentery. A man by the name of William Nutter of New York went with them. He has been in California some years. It was he who hung those men of whom I spoke.[11] The excitement was great. Men left their work; all felt the necessity of some example. Murders were frequent. The proof against these men was to their minds clear. The most remarkable of the criminals was Captain Don Carlos, who fought for Mexico in the late war. Some said he had been a pirate of the South Seas. As they were about launching him into eternity he said, "what are you going to do with me?" "Hang you for your crimes." He responded, "hang and be d----." These were his last words. Nutter this evening gave us an account of the massacre of the Indians last winter.[12] Some Indians killed several miners; immediately the rest of the miners were determined on a desperate revenge. Wherever an Indian was found he was slaughtered; hundreds fell, the rest fled to the mountains. Here their suffering were great, their scanty stores were left in the flight. Some of the whites more human than we generally find under like circumstances went out to tell them that if they behaved themselves they need be under no apprehension for the future. One squaw that was married to a white man by the name of Smith they carried back on a litter. She had went to see her brother (who was a chief) when the attack was made, and on account of race dared not return home. Her husband was not with the party that went to induce the Indians to return. At present the population, though heterogeneous enough, appears to have none of those desperate characters. I have seen Chinese in their national costume; they seem intelligent and worthy.[13] One of them had served in India under the British flag. There are some Chileans here; they are but a few removes from the Indian.[14] Many of the miners are sailors, but I see nothing, as far as conduct is concerned, to distinguish them from the rest. I have conversed with several who were engaged in the whale fisheries. Their anecdotes are highly exciting. If the weather keeps fair we must get to work and prospect. I hear of some doing middling well. We may feel pleased we are not farther north. We can see the mountains; they appear like a vast collection of snow.

DECEMBER 2: Weather continues fine, though somewhat variable. I have made a cradle which works well. Drake and myself have worked several days near our cabin and made not more than two to three dollars. This would not do. Now we are working two miles up the stream near an Indian encampment. Our prospect is a little better. Yesterday we made about five dollars. Small work this; others are doing no better.

DECEMBER 9: During the past week the nights were very frosty, the days clear and pleasant. These Indians are classed among the lowest of the race. They are more degraded than any I have seen. In stature five feet six or seven inches, heavy set and well formed: featured more like the African than Indian. Formerly they were naked, or nearly so. Some of our men saw a considerable number of men and women in a nude state screaming and crying around a fire in which they were burning rags. This seems to be a religious ceremony to appease the Great Spirit when there is sickness or death among them. The women do all the work. I see them daily going to gather acorns and can constantly hear them pounding in a kind of mortar formed by a hollow in a rock. The labor is hard, their pestles weighing from ten to fifteen pounds. Some of them work entirely naked. They are well-made, muscular ladies, hands and feet small, ankles and wrists also small, but countenances anything except pleasing. Acorns are almost their only dependence for bread. They is gathered in large baskets which is swung on the woman's back and fastened by a band that passes over her shoulders and presses against her forehead. In this way they carry very heavy burdens; their children are also carried in the same manner, the weight being borne by the forehead. Some of the men work in the mines and have purchased clothes, and are well dressed, others having a shirt only. Perhaps a pair of pants a world to large, stockings and no shoes; woolen pants and cotton shirts, anything and everything. A woman is pretty well dressed in an old shirt, and very well if a blanket. A day or two since six boys were playing on a bank; three were naked, two with shirts, and the other had a silk handkerchief tied around him. Their huts are made of sticks and bark, a poor defense against the storm. I have heard many of them sing; their tunes seem almost uniform, quick, deep, and gutteral. They would be famous chaps to dance jigs. But they are men, and circumstances have made them what they are. The excitement of the chase and war (an Indian's school) they seem to know but little of. They have but a few bows and yet fewer guns. Their only constant companion is a knife. This week we made $67.50, our best week's work in California. One man on Weaver Creek within a mile of us had one hundred dollars per day for several days. Another at Hangtown took out $294, somewhat in that area. Provisions are falling in price owing to this dry weather.

DECEMBER 16: Made thirteen dollars Monday. Tuesday S. Giles and J. Gardner came to see us from North Fork. We went to the Long Canyon with them to see Graham and Gardner who were working there. It is a deep, rocky, dismal looking place. Our men have worked several days and made nothing. Paine, Giles, and company have made twenty dollars per day ever since they commenced work.[15] They are in much better place than we are. Graham and Joshua Gardner went with them; they have went to see if it would be best to move this winter. Hugh Dixon went to Sacramento city. Saw Wilson, who has passed through some trying scenes with Indians, bears, and panthers, but he escaped unhurt and is in enjoyment of excellent health. Six of our company are wintering in the city. There expenses are high and, from what I can learn, their income is considerably lighter. Wilson has received several letters from home, two of which he sent to Drake. This is the first news from home. All my family well. What pleasure does these five words give; showing at once how easy it is to confer a favor and create an obligation. But death has visited our friends. Mr. Day, one of Athen's best and most useful citizens, is no more. A friend of man and a consistent advocate of freedom, he lived to benefit his race. Mr. Gibbs, one whom I regarded, has went the way of all the earth. Lancaster, the would-be murderer, is in

Sacramento. Jenkins and family are at Salt Lake.[16] Lancaster is practicing law; in him Justice has a worthy advocate truly. On Tuesday it commenced to rain and has continued almost without interruption. One cannot wonder now what washes down the golden sands.

DECEMBER 23: Wednesday fair. Every other day except Saturday wet. The weather has been very mild for this latitude; but little frost at night and none in the day and, though here considered uncommonly wet, I was led by writers to expect more rain. Gardner has gone to North Fork. At present there is but little done in mining. Last week a Yankee found a piece weighing seventeen ounces. Yesterday we worked in the same ravine. Part of my time while it was raining I occupied in mending boots and shoes for some of our neighbors—$1.50 and they find the leather is not considered high for half-soling. I have read several romances. One only good, the *Trapper's Bride*.[17] Nearly all the novels I have seen either on the road or in California were written by depraved minds. A great many brought books of the first class, but generally they were discarded on account of weight. We have quite a number on our shelf, mostly medical and magazines: Knickerbocker's and Blackwood's, a biography of great men, Lyell's *Geology*, two on philosophy, and others, as the merchant says, too numerous to mention.[18] Evening fine.

DECEMBER 30: Some begin to think spring is opening. Those that have been here some years say this would not be without precedent, but it sounds so strange I don't believe it. Four of our men have gone to North Fork. They left on Thursday, the only wet day in the week. Christmas was a beautiful day. This week we feel like being in California; we made over two hundred dollars. On Wednesday in the p.m. we made sixty-eight dollars. The whole mining district is mountainous, and the richest places are generally in the deepest chasms or ravines. Sometimes, however, large quantities are deposited at the head of ravines where there is scarcely a depression. The gold in ravines having been washed but a small distance is often coarse and somewhat fantastic in appearance. I saw two lumps picked up near us worth ten dollars each. I found one worth some four to five dollars. Of the latter kind is one I saw nearly the shape of a heart. I also heard of a piece having a manifest likeness of the female head with hair neatly done up. It is often mixed with quartz, as if studded with diamonds. The quartz is exceedingly handsome, often appearing like a rose in its first bloom. We often see large quantities of this beautiful rock. I have been forcibly struck by one curiosity here we almost daily see; trees perforated through the bark and filled with acorns. Some trees are literally covered. The industrious laborer must be the woodpecker. I saw some time since a dead California eagle, one of the grandest of the feathered race. This day I saw a garden. It is said the Indians are beginning to remove to summer quarters.

January 6. Time, time, where art thou? Time is an ever flowing stream which washes all earth's sons away. As I look back on my journey many, very many, whom I knew have sunk beneath the wave. They, like me, wished for life and sought happiness; but their friends almost forget them, the place that knew them knows them not. The busy crowd passes on; they are not missed no more than if they were yet alive, or never had been born. The sun rises, the world is illuminated, and man is rejoiced. The earth feels his warmth and turns with busy life. The young child and the young lamb alike skip about and are glad. The future, like a track-less ocean, may have rocks and quicksands, storms, tempests, but fear not; He who knows the future has left a chart to guide and we shall triumph when time shall be no more.

A few nights since I thought in my dream my spirit was permitted to return and see those whom it loves. (I saw them much more distinctly than I could in moments of conscious-ness.) Fancy bade them farewell and took its flight. The weather for the past week has been variable. This is here the season for grass. Many places are now green which I have seen destitute of even the appearance of vegetation. The soap plant, which I have mentioned, I find very numerous. It grows with a leaf like a flag, having black fibers to support the leaves. When the leaves decay, these fibers unite about the bulb and close over it. To me, this process appears to last for years as some are very large in comparison to the smallest I have seen, being not larger than a nutmeg. Of the former, some are two inches to three in diameter, oval and tapering towards the end. A considerable quantity of the oak is of the genius live, as their plentiful foliage attests. It looks like black oak but burns as well as white. Green pine is a non-conductor of heat.

JANUARY 10: Constant rain since Monday. The streams are swollen. Winter is in California yet. At the last rain Sacra-mento was threatened with a flood, in some places the water was three feet deep. The present rain must be more destruc-tion to property. Diseases of stomach and bowels, I learn, are very generally fatal and sickness prevalent.

JANUARY 13: Yet rainy. Drake is unwell and has been for some days. Heavy cold is the cause. His bones ache and his teeth are loose. Calomel lurking in his system is probably in some measure chargeable with a part. One evening last week we had rice for supper, of which I made a hearty meal. It tasted rather fantish (having nothing but sugar on it). Some time afterwards in the night I stept to the door; the cold air caused a strange sensation, my shoulders struck the bake oven and fortunately saved my head from a severe blow against the fireplace. Returning consciousness made me feel rather uneasy. This was the only time in fifteen years that I fainted. At present well.

JANUARY 20: January this far has been a hard month. December generally pleasant, but this month is a pretty fair representative of winter. On Monday night snow fell to the depth of two or three inches. In many places, however, the earth was bare in the morning. The thickest ice so far scarcely one-half inch. Frost generally white. If the sun shines the days are warm, but some days are dark and very chilly. The earth soon dries after a heavy rain as it is principally a kind of limey-looking gravel, I suppose decomposed granite. A little snow on Thursday. Yesterday was the coldest I have seen in California. The winter is considered uncommonly severe. The rains and floods greater than in twenty years. In speaking of Sacramento, I said its history might be brief. The late freshet has brought the water up to six feet on the highest ground occupied. Tents of course were removed and many of the houses are ruined. All other towns, except San Francisco, are injured. The bridge at Coloma has been swept away. At present the atmosphere evidently indicates an approaching storm. We are continually inquiring of the mail. There is and has been sad disorder. It seems at present a folly to expect a letter. We gave our names six weeks since to a forwarding concern, and no return from the express yet.

Even the love of gain might spur; $2.50 for a letter. Have not heard of the message yet. The rains no doubt partly the cause. Both pretty well.

JANUARY 25: This week this far has been almost one continued shower of snow or rain. Monday and Tuesday and Wednesday constant snow, since then rain. Here the snow melted very fast, at no time deeper than six inches. Other places toward the mountains the depth is wonderful. Thirty miles from this place, on the Middle Fork, snow six feet deep, on the Sierra Nevada the trees cannot be seen, which leads me to think the depth over fifty feet. A young man in coming from North Fork found some places bare. As he ascended a mountain (the dividing ridge), he found snow gradually increased to the depth of eight inches; at the base on either side none. He says the North Fork in one night rose twenty-five feet, destroying everything within reach. Sad news; five men working on a bar went to sleep as usual in their tent, little dreaming of the morrow. In the morning they were standing in water vainly expecting succor. Fortune seemed to favor; a log came near, they sprang on it, but the water was not to be deprived of its prey, the log turned and they sank to rise no more.

JANUARY 27: Went over to Coloma to buy potatoes. Bought at seventy-five cents per pound, here $1.50 is asked. Saw some wild cattle drove across the river. They were as wild as deer, but not quite as nimble. Several of them broke from the herd, but the Spaniards soon brought them to a sense of the law of necessity. Presently two beautiful white fellows burst and ran at the top of their speed and took different routes, but with the same grand objective—liberty. The race was even for some time between horse and ox, but the lasso soon ended the unequal strife. Each unfortunate was caught and tied, then left to waste his strength in fruitless efforts to rise. This breaks their spirit. None but Spaniards can drive them. Beef is selling at thirty-seven to fifty per pound. Went to the mill-race where the gold was first seen. Saw a Mr. Marshall who claims the discovery.[19] Inquired if a letter might have strayed there searching for me. "None." Newspapers very late for sale; November only one dollar. Read one of October. Poor Hungary! It seems she is at the mercy of the hungry maul of Russia. And poor France! Crazy as ever. What remedy will she try next? No important news from the States.

FEBRUARY 3: Went to the mill again for potatoes. Scurvy must have some enemy to divert its attention so that we may escape. Roads beginning to be good. Great numbers starting in pursuit of better diggings. Nearly all seem to be unsettled in their minds. Some have gone up in the mountains through four feet of snow, each person expecting that by being among the first he may secure a rich placer. We must move soon. Brought a letter to send home by a Cincinnatian.

The American River

February 10—August 11

[On reaching California the Buckeye Rovers scattered throughout the mining district; some worked that fall and winter on the main rivers, others found permanent residences for the duration of the wet season. Banks, Drake, Reeves, and Townshend erected a cabin in Cold Spring, where they prospected until the return of warm, dry weather when they joined the rush to the high streams, restricting their activities to the upper two forks of the American River.]

FEBRUARY 10: Spring appears to be coming in good ernest. The reign of heat and drought are about to be reinstated in place of chilly rains. Tomorrow Mr. Morrow and Green Buler (two men living in a cabin near us) and myself start for the city to buy mules to pack to Middle Fork.[1]

Dixon and Ferrill have come over from North Fork. Generally speaking men have done well, a few remarkably well. One man found a lump weighing sixteen pounds. Graham has been sick most of the time, exposure and fatigue the cause. All the company there propose going to Yuba as the reports are uncommonly flattering. Dixon and Ferrill came to see about some property, goods, or chattels they had here. They will return in a day or two.

FEBRUARY 17: Returned after a very hard week. Took cold the first night; the change from a log cabin and bedstead to a cloth hotel and the floor was more than I could bear. I felt very unwell most of the time since. Wednesday morning when we came in the city I felt my whole system ache. Shortly a desperate chill that made my knees strike and my teeth to chatter seemed to say, "fear for the future." I went to bed. To be sick in a tavern away from home and dear friends, surrounded by men whose sole objective is gain, anywhere is miserable, in California it is horrible. For three hours I felt fever quickening my pulse, but gradually felt better when a gentle sweat broke the spell that held my mind perhaps more than my body. My spirits revived, not that fear was monarch, but who that thinks could feel composed in a vile, filthy city when half the houses stand over stagnant water. Next day I was able to attend to business. Bought two mules at three hundred and fifty dollars, one for Drake and myself and one for Reeves and Townshend. Bought flour at eleven dollars per hogshead. Prices are low compared to a few weeks since. Despite the flood the place has wonderfully improved. The pasteboard and cloth houses have been nearly all washed from their places, but the number of good frame buildings speaks something like permanent improvement.[2] There are many vessels at the levee. Nothing strikes the visitor like the vast piles of lumber all the way from the Kennebec round the Horn. Well done, Mr. Yankee! Left on Friday, stopt the first night at a Mr. Whiteside's. We had butter and milk, victuals cooked by a decent and neat woman. Once more within the pale of civilization. Got home this day. I felt very weak coming up.

FEBRUARY 24: The past has been a stormy and very disagreeable week. I never saw snow fall faster or weather more variable, snow, hail, and rain in thirty minutes. Winter yet.

January had but five dry days and February is going out stormy.

On Monday Drake took a load to Middle Fork, but on account of the weather stopt at Greenwood Valley eight miles from the mill. He and those that were with him came back satisfied they had ventured out too soon. Hear the Message is in California and a slaveholder, as usual, speaker. So might it be.

MARCH 3: Raining and snowing, with occasional glimpses of a bright hot sun. This day is much like the week just gone. Each day we were flattered with sunshine, but disappointed by showers, and consequently did nothing. I have a miserable bad cold on my lungs. It annoys me night and day. I heated myself hunting for mules and incautiously exposed myself. Hear of many hiring, wages from five to eight dollars per day and found there is much uncertainty in mining. Some of those who design returning next fall, and many of another class that have much fear and but little enterprise, think a bird in hand worth two in the bush.

George Reeves went to the city last week as witness against a Mr. Hicks who claimed one thousand dollars for medical attendance on a family in a neighborhood where no person heard of his being an M.D. Here the Indians are chasing one of their tribe to shoot him. He had murdered one of their number.

MARCH 10: Weather yet unfavorable. Many who went north some weeks since are returning. They say there is too much water to work. Hear that three murdered bodies have been found on the opposite side of the river from Sacramento city. Mr. Buler of Missouri, with whom we expect to be in company next summer, had one brother-in-law murdered on one of the streams, and another who died in Sacramento having one thousand dollars and upwards. The robber in whose home he died refuses to give any account of it. Law might reach him but the cost would devour the principal.

Last week there was great excitement among the Indians. They say a white man shot one of them, cause not known. Some white beings, doubting their own manhood and courage, speak of life in general and that of Indians' in particular, very lightly. Such think if their hands are once stained with human blood their title to knighthood indisputable. One chap that had agreed with a company to drive them on shares sold wagon and team, then immediately gambled away the price, six hundred dollars. My health much improved. Anxiety to hear from home sometimes almost overpowers me. Some disagreeable dreams of my brother Robert trouble me. I hope they are vain shadows of vain thought.

MARCH 17: Yesterday was the only day without heavy rain since this day last week. Sacramento is probably flooded again. Three times this winter Sacramento, like Amsterdam, might be traversed in all directions in boats. There is much grand scenery in this country. Every stream is a torrent, waterfalls innumerable. The grandest falls I ever viewed is that of Hangtown Creek where it leaps in two bounds two hundred feet into Weaver. In the summer it is nearly dry, at present almost a river.

Spring seems at length here. Some of the trees are putting forth leaves and the birds building their nests. There are but few songsters here that warble forth songs of love. The pigeon and wild goose have come to build homes for their summer broods. I suppose they think California what the Icelander says of his home, the best land the sun shines on. Read the

President's message, think it a cautious, well written document.[3]

Spent some of my time in reading Walker's six letters.[4] Though I had read them formerly, yet their force and simplicity to me appears wonderful. For the first time I one day last week looked over a package of extracts Maria cut from some newspapers for me. Some of the poetry is very beautiful.

MARCH 24: At last the monotony of a camp life is broken. We left on Wednesday. Roads better than expected, weather yet unsettled. Sent two on to prospect as high up on Middle Fork as possible. Their report is favorable, gold somewhat plenty. A part of the road over five feet of snow. Notwithstanding, we intend to start tomorrow morning. On Wednesday evening we reached Greenwood Valley where we are at present encamped. This valley owes its name to a half-breed named Greenwood. This unfortunate wretch was recently found dead under a tree; liquor was his executioner. Spent one day hunting our animals, scarcely expected to find them. In the evening we found them about three miles back on the road. This species of property is so uncertain few men expect to see an animal again if a few hours out of sight. Horse thieves are not very plenty, but mule thieves seem almost as numerous as mules. Men are trying to make money by every means.

This week S. Townshend left us. Went back to Cold Spring. Leaving a cabin seems rather hazardous. We have an oil cloth to spread on the ground. All of us are well and in good spirits. Distance fifteen miles north by west of Cold Spring.

MARCH 31: The past has been a week of hard labor and some

little misfortune. We are now encamped in a valley thirteen miles north of Greenwood. Crossed Middle Fork three times. The mountains descending and ascending are a mile or upwards in length each and some two thousand feet high. The river is full of rapids. At present it is rising fast, the ferry man says ten feet in four days. The boat is about sixteen feet long and eight wide, having sailings. It is propelled by means of a rope fastened across the stream, which is placed behind two blocks secured to the boat. Two men then force it across by pulling the rope. While standing on the top of one of these mountains I thought the view one of the wildest and grandest in nature. We who are toiling through these mountains may be sick of such sights, yet artists will delight the world with views taken in this region. Saw S. Bowers of Zanesville working in a ravine this side of Middle Fork. Our misfortune is this; Wednesday evening we turned out our animals to feed, on Thursday morning we commenced to look for them. From that to the present time we can hear neither tale nor tiding of them. Some rain today. The snow is disappearing fast. About here nearly all is gone. Our situation is very comfortable.

APRIL 6: Hunted five days for our animals, in the meantime offered five dollars reward for each. A man found them in a deep canyon near the river. Packed up our effects to a mountain over a canyon we had hoped to work in—thirteen miles. The rush up this way is tremendous. Much gold has been dug in this vicinity and doubtless a vast amount will be taken out this season by crowd after crowd, almost one continuous stream of men. Every place is snatched up in a moment. This canyon is claimed to its very head, nearly twenty miles, each man being allowed but twenty feet. Each man's name is recorded and he leaves pick or shovel at his claim. If absent on the first of June, any other man can take his place. At present the water is too high for him to know whether the bottom is smooth rock or has the least appearance of gold. All is bustle, confusion, and anxiety. Many with dark brows trying to discourage all they can. Packers have packed up large quantities of provisions until they have knocked the market ruinously low for them; flour fifty cents, pork seventy-five. A few weeks since flour was $1.25. Here there is not a particle of grass for our animals. Morrow and myself start this afternoon for Sacramento to sell. We may need them yet, but we have no alternative, five dollars per day would scarcely feed one here.

APRIL 15: This day returned. We had a very hard time. It rained two days as we were going. Arrived at the city on Tuesday, the ninth, just a year since we left home. I had asked Drake in what way we might commemorate this day. Little did I expect to enjoy the most agreeable way in the world by reading a letter from *Home*. O, what pleasure to read over and over again those lines traced by the hand of affection. All well and happy but for my absence. What more could I wish? William Booth and family safely across the raging ocean.[5] I am content, but no, would that I were there. As a bird to her nest, or a needle to the pole, so turn I toward home.

The Sacramento and American were very full. The city was in constant dread of inundation. Every means was tried to keep it out but their levee, thrown up in the face of the water, may delay but cannot prevent. The water was some four feet higher than some of the best of the city. Merchants were removing their goods to the vessels for safety. This made all kinds of business dull. Animals fell in price, I got but one hundred fifty dollars for a mule I gave two hundred dollars for. Here, like all other places, it is hard to keep money. Low as provisions are, some yet ask two dollars per meal; near the city a dollar fifty, and in the city one dollar. The number of houses about being opened is wonderful. Near every running stream the traveler sees canvas stretched and liquor for sale. The appearance of the plain is most surprising. Last fall and early this spring the earth seemed sterile. It seemed impossible to call this part of California beautiful. Nature, as if to atone for the drought of summer, has now arrayed those plains in the most beautiful flowers. It seems as if every variety were here, from the small flower just seen in the grass to the large scarlet that flaunts before the sun. To me it seemed like fairy land. All nature looked gay.

In Sacramento there is much to admire; its rapid growth, its bustling enterprise. Here the Yankee shows his true character almost better than in his own New England. You know him in a moment by his restless, enterprising appearance. The landing is piled up with the fruits of his industry: houses ready framed to be converted into tenements in the shortest notice, boards planed, and sashes packed up by the dozen. Cloth houses are replaced by substantial buildings. One of the best looking houses in town, called the Humboldt, is the headquarters for gambling. Perhaps a dozen tables laden with silver to the amount of four to five thousand dollars.[6] One wonders where the money came from, yet this is only one perhaps of one hundred. Up here two gamblers who had been warm friends by the names of White and Helmy quarreled; White shot Helmy, and Helmy's brother stabbed White. They both died in a few seconds.

APRIL 21: Another week spent in fruitless effort. Rained on

Friday. Air cold, snow fell quite near. Drake and Reeves went ten miles up to Canyon Creek. All taken up. Their journey desperately toilsome, down some mountains so steep they had to catch the brush to prevent falling. Went to work in canyon we thought might be overlooked. (Here we have Mr. Bowers as a partner.) Prospect poor. Came to our old camp on the hill this morning.

APRIL 28: Encamped on the North Fork of Middle Fork. Here we expect our home this summer. Last Tuesday three of us came to see some men Morrow and Buler were acquainted with. They told us we might get a claim next below theirs. We have it, and so far consider ourselves lucky. On this stream a person cannot hold more than one claim. This was claimed by a person who went in as a partner in a claim above. It is said to be very rich. We are situated one mile below the mouth of the Rich Canyon, yet we had to come four miles around. We now felt what it is to turn mule. We have packed three loads, some forty pounds each. The road is one that to be known must be seen, up one mountain and down one, two miles long and not less than five thousand feet high. Within some one thousand feet of the creek the trail is dug, winding from side to side, otherwise it would be almost impossible to travel it. Steep as it is, mules bring two hundred pounds down. On Tuesday we came down the canyon, some places where we crossed the bluffs made me tremble. One false step and all would be over. Death seemed suspended by a hair. The mountains are rugged and wild in the extreme.

MAY 5: A week of hard toil. We packed down our summer's provisions, each of us carrying fifty pounds on two days in succession. I have carried seven loads altogether down this mountain. The excitement about finding good diggings is wonderful. Men talk of getting gold by the pound. Went into the hills over the Eldorado Canyon, where we had been encamped, expecting some letters as some packers promised to be up from Sacramento and bring anything there might be in the office for us. Not up yet. Saw Bowers has a claim in Secret Canyon (so-named because many made fruitless efforts to find it). Says some New York men in a few weeks last fall dug ten thousand dollars each. He starts in the morning for Deer Creek dry diggins to work until the first of July. At present the snow in this canyon is from ten to thirty feet in depth. One place it is bridged with snow, though the stream is some thirty feet wide. In Deer Creek dry diggins some men last fall tied the legs of their pants to make sacks and carried off one hundred twenty-five pounds, so says Bowers. Other stories equally wild are told, seemingly in good faith. All are in wild excitement, or calmly waiting for the water to fall that they may jump and catch the gold.

MAY 12: This day spent in a way not the most agreeable. I attended a meeting of the miners of this district, which embraces all working on this river. The object of the meeting to elect an alcalde and make such regulations as might be thought advisable.[7] Earlier in the season a similar meeting had been held when but few were on this stream. Now the cooperation of all was requested. Sunday is perhaps the only day men could be brought together. On this day but few work. Strange to witness, several men of intelligent appearance were loud in praise of mob law as more expeditious, more economical. In short, every way the best. This I opposed and had the pleasure to find a majority for what I deemed right. The meeting would compare favorably with some I have elsewhere seen. The path down the river to the place of meeting, some four miles, is on the side of the mountain, in many places one false step would precipitate a person many feet over rocks into the river. Wrote home this week and to Jane and Cornelius.[8] Worked none. Weather somewhat cool. Snow not melting as fast as we wish. Heard considerable encouragement as to our prospect in mining. Received a letter from Jane and Cornelius.

MAY 19: The weather is delightful, the atmosphere dry and bracing. The middle of the day is as warm as midsummer in Ohio. Sometimes clouds appear and rain seems about to fall. One day the sun was surrounded by a very dark circle (one would say a very sure sign of rain), but in a short time nothing could be seen except a thickness, or milky appearance of the air like Indian Summer. We worked three days and made fifty dollars; small work for five. Drake was sick. The water begins to fall and the time for hard work drawing near.

This day, when circumstances permit, I occupy in this manner: the forenoon principally in reading the Scriptures and meditation; in the afternoon I read my letters and review the past week. When I look at the flight of time and think what a few years has done, I am astonished to be here where but a short time since all was still except the occasional sound of a savage might echo through these wilds. Now filled by thousands of men whose only love seems to be gold. Yet the next few years will witness a far more awful state of society. Abandoned women seem necessary to make men fiends. These are arriving by thousands and spreading through the mines.[9] In San Francisco fifty to one hundred dollars will buy one. Gambling now is mated.

MAY 26: Went up to Secret Canyon, went all around the heads of the Eldorado and within some thirty miles of the

Sierra Nevada. Traveled many miles on snow one to five feet deep. Saw the snow bridge, but the stream is not more than one-half of thirty feet, almost impossible to walk through. Out three nights. Snowed and rained very hard for a time on Thursday. Frost every night. Could buy a claim for twenty-five dollars, fifty feet, but think best to confine ourselves to this. Appearance of gold good, but no certainty. Quartz in large quantities. Five with me, but one of our company. The snow is melting fast and yet there is some fifteen feet deep that I stood near. Three weeks since all the brush that we found so annoying was covered; snow then was five to ten feet on a level. On Thursday thunder and lightning, almost the only I have heard in California.

We walked on some ridges thousands of feet high, in some places so narrow two men could not go abreast. Mountains steep each side, but these mountains differ very much from the Rockies. There you see ranges principally of solid rock; here earth vastly predominates, making the mountains seldom precipitous. The prevailing rock here is slate, granite also, with seams of quartz. Saw but one deer and no other kind of game. Indians seem all gone from this region. Waters falling. All in good health.

JUNE 2: This time a year since we were pushing along Platte, straining every nerve to pass all teams near us. "Go ahead," our motto, little thinking what the latter part of the journey would be. Our ears were open for the least word relative to California. A year past and but little done. Thousands, I suppose, are now urging their way through mud and water, dust, and ashes for California, California. Men are getting to work in the Eldorado, and do not find it as rich as anticipated, yet there is too much water for a fair trial. Tomorrow we intend to commence to make plank for a part of our race.[10] Got two axes ground; one dollar each for the use of a grindstone, two dollars for the use of a cross-cut saw per day, also two dollars for the use of a broad-axe per day, and sixteen dollars if it is injured. This is one way to make money.

For herding horses and mules, four dollars per week or fifteen dollars per month, and not accountable even at that. For bringing a letter from the city, two dollars and fifty cents, or one down, fifty cents. Satinette pants ten dollars, socks of poor quality one dollar fifty cents. Provisions on the same key; a fat ox two hundred dollars (some have been packed up and then killed), demand constant. Cheese a dollar fifty per pound, raisins the same, potatoes one dollar, and dried apples one dollar. Liquor plentiful at twenty-five cents per dram. I have not tasted the article in nearly three months.

JUNE 9: Tuesday George Reeves went upon the mountain and to our no small surprise and delight found Dewing and Earheart.[11] They are well. Drake was very much tired, hard work seems a very difficult task for him. He has gone to Sacramento to try his fortune. Dewing is made of sterner stuff and seems not easily disheartened. It is almost impossible to tell what pleasure we have enjoyed in hearing of home and all our neighbors. The little gossip and ready answers to each question showed that with all man's improvements there is nothing like the tongue yet. They brought letters and mailed them at sea, so it is doubtful that we shall ever see them. Drake received a letter March 23rd. All well. John C. Calhoun is no more. A great mind sadly perverted to an unworthy objective, a blasphemer of Freedom in her own Temple. Stopt to kill a snake that was among our dishes, within four feet of the tent. It is about three feet long and not more than one and a half inches in diameter; color very bright black and white spotted like a copperhead. Killed a small rattlesnake two weeks since. Some have been killed that were quite large. Lizzards are very numerous. The frilled lizzard is a great curiosity.

The water has fallen some five inches in the last week. Dewing and Earheart have been some time searching for a place to locate, but all is claimed. Some men have a half dozen or more claims, intending to speculate. A man told me he had been near the summit of the Sierra Nevada and that every place having the least appearance of gold was claimed. One individual perhaps claims one thousand feet of a stream, sticks up his notice "A.B. and Company (no telling how large that is) claim this stream up or down." Some places miners regulate this matter. On this stream, from its mouth to Eldorado, a company may take as much of this stream as they can drain. On the bars twenty feet square is all a man can claim; on Middle Fork but ten. The pretense of taking claims in the manner above described is to wait for low water, but at best it is only to try to be sure of the best. Decent men, to avoid strife, will respect them but others will not. It is somewhat amusing to see the poor fellows when they first arrive in the mines. How sadly disappointed they are; can't see a speck of gold what six or seven feet of dirt and rocks, and then not sure. O, if I had known this before I left home! [12] You did not tell us of the thousands that make nothing. No, but you told us of the big lumps. D——— such a country as this, if I can only get out, that's all!

JUNE 16: This climate is surely strange, the past week has been as cold and cloudy as I have ever seen in the States at this season. Some rain on Tuesday and a few drops several times since. Snow nearly all gone and the sun gradually regaining his old dominion. Vegetation springs up and opens her eyes after a long nap; for a short time she will look happy and gay like a bride in her honeymoon. The flowers are now fading on the plains. Here there are but few flowers and yet fewer birds. The turtle dove breathes forth her soft mourn. This is the only bird I know. The lofty pines are the most beautiful objects we view—cedar, pitch spruce, and white pine. Everywhere throughout the mines there are more or less of these noble trees. Wild as this region is, it has but few wild animals, except deer and wolves. I have seen nothing larger, though I occasionally hear of a grizzly. One broke a man's arm so that he was forced to have it amputated. Within a few miles of us, in the ridge between here and North Fork of the American, a panther was killed measuring twelve feet from the tip of his nose to the end of the tail a short time since, and also what is called a California lion seen near the mountains. Grizzlies are decidedly dangerous citizens. Dewing, I guess, will stay on this stream. Drake got four letters, I none. Last night dreamed I was home and felt sadly perplexed to know how I came; determined to return, but thought all must be a dream. Night before thought father was dead.

JUNE 23: At this moment there is one of the most awful exhibitions of the affect of drunkeness that I have ever witnessed. A poor depraved mortal with a knife in his hand seeming to thirst for blood. O humanity, how art thou fallen! We were down to see Dewing, he has bought a share in a claim at one hundred fifty dollars, eight in the company. There is one of the most marvelous stories in circulation, even for this marvelous land. Some one hundred miles from here a lake has been discovered so rich as justly to entitle it to the name of Golden Lake.[13] Fortunes are made in a few days. Thousands are flocking and, were I persuaded of its truth, of course I should be off. But Eldorado has failed, and Secret Canyon has lost its charm. All is not gold that glitters. My mind at times is tranquil and I feel as if certain of returning next winter; at other times I feel dejected, weary, and saddened. Our situation is exceedingly trying, waiting measurably on uncertainties.

JUNE 30: Another week and nothing made, but we have much hard work done on our race. Some one hundred feet is dug, and one hundred twenty feet of sleepers laid for boards which are ready. The sides are to be canvas. It cost one dollar per yard, nails seventy-five a pound, and tacks a dollar and a half a paper. Some are trying to turn the river, but there is three or four times too much water yet. Last Monday I received three letters, two carried by Dewing and Earheart, and one from Cornelius and Jane. All well. The middle of the day very warm.

JULY 4: Fourth of July, what do you bring to my memory as my mind dances back and forth on the wires of time? The past, where is it? In gloomy forgetfulness? No, but in the living present, treasured near my heart. The pleasure of the past invites me to happiness (its sorrows are but few). In the distance I see the Future, solemn but not sad, with outstretched arm she beckons me forward; Hope, with her golden wings and beautiful countenance, stands smiling at her side and I boldly advance. Thirty-two years on the road of life. Where am I? What am I? And what might I have been? Or what will a few more years unfold? These are questions I cannot answer now. For dinner today we ate peaches which grow on trees shading my home.

JULY 7: Went up the mountain seeking for letters. Found none. I have scarcely ever found a greater conflict of emotions. I feel almost overpowered by the intensity of the struggle: home and friends, deep anxiety, hope and fear, in quick succession. How little control we possess over our busy inmate who is constantly comparing the present with the past, or perhaps sketching out some pleasing view of the future, but ending with there is but little certainty there. Without hope of immortality what is life?

JULY 9: Yesterday I saw a man who crossed the plains this spring. His company reached the diggings twenty-third instant, in sixty-six days from St. Joseph. A vast number are coming. Even this early there is much distress among emigrants. They saw large quantities of buffaloes, one grand sight a large herd feeding on the ridge between South and North Forks of Platte, just above Ash Hollow. They say that a majority of the dead interred last year have been dug up by the wolves; naked skulls and torn clothes the only monuments of the departed. They passed over forty miles of snow on Sierra Nevada.

The following lines taken from *The True Delta* possess one grand tract of beauty and truthfulness.

CALIFORNIA

by LADY EMMELINE STUART WORTLEY

What hurrying crowds have sought yon golden shore,
Far past the wide spread plain or ocean's roar;
Some to exult in rapture of success,
And speed once more to home and happiness

And some, alas, as ardent and as brave,
To sink and fade in an untimely grave!
For their expectant friends afar shall come,
With thunder shock, the tidings of their doom!
What to the sad survivor's aching breast
The wealth that cost that life they loved the best?
What unto them is all the gold that lines
Resplendent California's glowing mines?
For them its gifts were dirth—its gains but loss—
Through their fond tears its wealth seems worthless drops.
Yet California hath a treasure still
For those whose mourning hearts with anguish shrill,
But that lies buried in the early tomb,
Where all their hopes went down in midnight gloom
For them all valueless those glittering veins
That light the earth where sleep those dear remains!
Dearer to them that much loved honored mould
Than the bright region's gathered spoils of gold;
For them, indeed, its wealth has passed away,
And all its treasures is that mouldering clay!

I sometimes hear of some shocking barbarities. A young man of Hudson, New York, by the name of Esmond, told me the following. As he was walking on the valley about a mile from the banks of the Yuba, some thirty miles above its junction with Feather River, his attention was arrested by the appearance of a recent fire. On examination, to his horror-strickened eyes, appeared blood; the evidence of recent murder was fresh. In the ashes was a human skull and some bones partly calcined, also the sole of a shoe filled with hobnails. Near he found a legging. This is all he ever knew. To all who heard it, it was a mystery, followed by no examination, no search, each had his own business to attend and no time to waste on the dead. To me it is evident the murdered man was a foreigner, as indicated by the legging; most probably a native of Britain. He had been successful and was flushed with hopes of a happy reunion with beloved friends. Perhaps he had written that he was about to return. They look for him, but shall look in vain. He heeds them not. His secret is unknown except to some dark villain in whose heart it is hid.

JULY 14: Received a letter from home. All in the enjoyment of good health. Wrote an answer, but how to get it to Sacramento I know not. The water is at last in our race. We have had nearly three months hard labor and next to no pay. Now that the time is near when we shall see the result, I feel as if a weighty lawsuit were pending and I am very fearful of the result. My only evidence is circumstantial.

JULY 21: How strange that nearly all our thoughts should be of gold. Yet circumstanced as we are, this is a comprehensive word. We are not misers, yet gold speaks of home, friends, and every near and endearing connection. If our prospects brighten we feel cheerful, our eyes dance in delight. On the other hand, when clouds cross our path, the storm and tempest rage within until the sunshine of hope dispels the gloom. We are now about half between hope and fear. Mr. Dewing was here, feels discouraged. He and I sent letters home. Most of the claims are now being tested and seem to prove possession not like pursuit. Above us Robinson and company are doing middling well. All must work in water.

JULY 27: Yesterday I received a very bad bruise on my left leg just below the knee. It is badly swelled, somewhat blackened, and very numb. It will prevent me from being able to work for some days. The bed of the river is a succession of large stones and rocks. As we roll them up in heaps, it requires caution. A man below had his foot broken by the fall of one. The rock that crushed against me would weigh more than a half a ton. I have employed myself since in making a shirt. I am a middling good tailor, but it puzzles me how women can live on the niggerdly wages they receive. Little wonder they seek to arouse the nation to a sense of their numerous wrongs. It is laughable to see men thrown on their own resources. Cooking in many cases is miserable, but patching takes the lead. Old boots, legs, canvas, flour sacks, no matter what and, as for know how, it is like the patches. The Amazonians got along well enough without men; Californians are trying the opposite experiment. For my part, I may pronounce it a complete failure. Today we joined claims with the company next below us. They had backed water on us so we could not work. They seemed willing to accomodate and we thought best to work theirs first. By this arrangement ten work together; four of Ohio, two of New York, two of Missouri, one of Illinois, and one of Virginia. Well mixed.

JULY 28: Why do we think this day more than other days? On this day Christ arose from the dead. Why did He die? He died to save sinners. He offered himself a ransom for slaves bound hand and foot, sold to sin. God has accepted the ransom, and all who believe this great truth are Christ's freemen. God laid on Him the inequity of us all. By His stripes we who are wounded and bruised are healed. When we are weak, God laid our help on One that was mighty. He himself bore our sins in his own body on the tree. He arose to prove He was the Mighty God, the Everlasting Father, and the Prince of Peace, beyond the glittering, starry sky, which God's right hand sustains. There in the boundless realms of light, our Great Redeemer reigns.

AUGUST 4: Perhaps there are few places more calculated more to try the mind than this. Except we possess some brace or support when our fancied-with is dashed away, we would be prostrate. Few exerted themselves more than we. I have been to Sacramento twice, less to Secret Canyon; out in the rain and snow, through mud, and over deep snow, and what have we—nothing but a severe lesson well learnt. At the present time we do not know that we shall have a cent. Some are leaving this stream, and all are more or less disappointed. The large streams, as a general thing, are best. Early in the season men thought there must be large deposits in the mountains and all the most enterprising were on the alert. Some crossed the Sierra Nevadas several times. In short, every place was tried. One man would think he found a rich placer; others, learning of his secret, would magnify it, hence a rush. O here it is! O there it is! No mistake. How do you know? O, it was prospected last fall; two or three men took out ten or twenty thousand dollars then! Wait contented until the water falls. Presently all is claimed. Along comes a lot of poor fellows, well they are too late. See how disappointed they are. What a pleasant smile one side and a dejected frown on the other. He is forced to go back and content himself with some eight or ten dollars per day. Three or four months pass, how stands the balance now? He had one thousand dollars. We climb the mountain with a heavy heart and a light purse, some three or four hundred dollars worse than when the race began. Such is the history of many persons. Eldorado, Secret Canyon, South Fork of North Fork, North Fork of Middle Fork, perhaps not quite so bad yet bad enough. How many more I know not, these are all near. Some, however, find very good diggings. A Mr. Scott, keeping a store near us, won over one hundred dollars gambling today. Many, very many, will go home with long faces, very good men by the way and say, "see, I made one thousand dollars, I was industrious, I was fortunate, I had good diggings." Yes, you had gambling with drunken men. We intend to try this place a little longer. Lost four day's work, leg almost well.

AUGUST 11: No letters for us by this mail. We have a race four hundred eighty feet long in operation, yet our prospect is anything but encouraging. We joined interests with a company next below us. Their claim proved a failure, so we moved their canvas race. Very many are leaving this stream. Some claims prospected last fall and believed to be rich are being deserted. Ten of us made sixty-three dollars yesterday, poor pay in California.

Ophir

August 18—February 20

[With the start of the 1850 season Banks and his associates joined
the rush to the Middle Fork of the American. Succumbing to the
general optimism of the time they acquired a claim, constructed
an elaborate sluice, and waited for the water to recede so they
could gather up the gold. When tested in the latter part of July,
the placer proved a failure. That year the Middle Fork yielded
little gold. The Ohioans then moved on to North Fork, joining
thousands of miners from every river and stream in the never-
ending search for the lucky strike.]

AUGUST 18: Writing once more on the roadside, not in search
of California, but of good diggings. I am now sitting on the
ridge between North and Middle Forks, near their junction,
not knowing exactly where to move. We have left our claim
like hundreds of others. We meet them from Yuba and
Feather, and almost every stream. Misery loves company; we
have plenty, but the more the worse prospect. Sometimes I
feel almost distracted.

Emigrants are coming in very numerously. They report
great distress on Humboldt, some starved to death, and
others have drowned themselves to escape like fate. The mortality on Platte greater than last year, ten to one. Humboldt
is so high they cannot get their animals to grass. Dead cattle
in heaps on the roads for three hundred miles. Thirteen men
crossed the Sierra Nevadas, six killed by Indians.

AUGUST 25: North Fork at Oregon Bar. We don't travel very fast but we keep moving. The last week we were at South Fork, which we found principally occupied by Dutch, except in the neighborhood of Salmon Falls.[1] Every place is dug up so that the prospect is gloomy. Two to eight dollars per day is about the wages. With the fall of labor in California everything else seems to sympathize. Provisions are quite low: flour sixteen cents to eighteen, pork twenty-five to fifty, potatoes eighteen to twenty-five, other articles in proportion. Prospecting is a necessity and a dangerous business. It is hard to adjust the balance between low wages and the loss of time and expenses of prospecting. He that is constantly in pursuit of good diggings will most assuredly never find them. Many men will tell you they have been to Trinity, Feather River, and Yuba, and found nothing, perhaps a year spent in this way. Nothing short of an ounce would do him. While he was spending his time and wasting his strength in fruitless efforts, a friend of his not able to endure the exposure and toil has been working for some six or eight dollars per day; one curses California, the other blesses it.[2] That man has his mind in the most torturing suspense, I might almost say agony; his friend is happy. The smiles of a grateful and affectionate family shall shortly crown his joys. But if each man is guided solely by his sense of duty, he stands acquitted to his own mind.

A fool may see the error of the past, but to weigh well the future is a difficult task for any man. In leaving Cold Spring we felt guided by the best information and, buoyed up by hope, endured many hardships, but we erred. Others came and worked a ravine running in front of our cabin and done well. We saw a man who was but a few days from there. The mines are not as extensive as was imagined. New dry diggings may be discovered, but in the rivers the best is gone. It is astonishing with what pertinacity men defend what they call their property. In Shirt Tail Canyon (Drake and Reeves were in it prospecting; it is above Birds on the Eldorado), nine men were damming the stream.³ This interfered with some men above who were digging in the banks. They came to tear away the dam; the company told them they would defend it with their lives, each party armed. The nine waited their return and shot thirteen who were in the act of tearing away the dam. Those who were to defend their run, the nine, were uninjured. Two gentlemen on Murderer's Bar, five miles above on Middle Fork, quarreled and agreed to settle it according to Don Quixote; fortunately their hands shook so badly they did not hit. This is one of the last evidences of civilization being in these parts.

SEPTEMBER 1: This day went to Murderer's Bar which is perhaps one of the richest places in California.⁴ Last winter it was first discovered to be a placer. As might be expected, in a few days every inch was claimed. The amount of work is truly astonishing that has been done, and large pay is yet expected in the river. They have a canvas race about ten feet wide made. A majority of the machines here used are quicksilver, the gold being very fine. As an illustration of the uncertainty of mining, take the following: An acquaintance of mine, Mr. Powell of Pennsylvania, owned a claim on this bar, and gave it to an old man who took out nine thousand dollars. Powell thought he could do better on North Fork of Middle Fork. He will probably make one thousand dollars. A man went up on Yuba, our creek, and went into land some person had left and took out nine thousand dollars. Two young men just across the plains dug seven hundred dollars in a few days on this stream where others had been digging all around the spot. Fickle fortune, she may smile someday, but a great many almost despair. The amount of labor thrown away on dams and ditches in California would make fifty or one hundred miles of railroad in Ohio. Received a letter from home today. All well, yet they could not quite fill the sheet. Too bad. The President is dead.[5] I wonder what effect this will produce. At Murderer's Bar I heard considerable quantities of quicksilver was found in the river connected with gold. It is found in small globules.

SEPTEMBER 8: We may feel sad because we are not fortunate. But what is our case? Happy thrice, happy compared to the poor emigrants. Their distress is horrible, some dying of starvation, others drowning themselves to escape like fate. The dead left unburied. Famine has done its complete work. Charity is not idle; perhaps one hundred thousand dollars has been raised, showing men here have souls. This past week a Mr. Avery, four weeks in California, broke his leg by falling from a bank. In twenty-four hours two hundred dollars were contributed for his relief. He said he did not expect such generousity. A contrast; Mr. McMeans has opened a hospital at Salmon Falls, twelve dollars required in advance, or security, per day. Our tramp down from the mountain, each carrying some twenty to thirty pounds, has caused two to be very sick—Green Buler and George Reeves. Buler is nearly well, Reeves is yet sick, their disease dysentery. I have seen a number of slaves here in California, a large majority of whom are struggling for freedom. One of Texas who expects to free himself, wife, and three children; New York or Massachusetts he intends his future home. A very smart fellow of Alabama says he wants no greater happiness than to be a *slave*. A man died on this bar a few days since by taking too much opium. Near here a man keeps a few cows; milk one dollar and twenty cents per quart. I expect to go on the hunt for winter diggings tomorrow. I had thought to be ready to return home.

A short time since, as I was stooping to drink at a spring, I was alarmed by hearing a merry tune near; as I drew back I saw a large rattlesnake within two feet of me.

SEPTEMBER 15: Another week lost prospecting. I have seen much of the country, but nothing very flattering. Some are coming forty miles to see diggings called "secret." (Here there is something in a name.) The gold is very fine, almost as fine as flour. Emigrants continue to come in in great distress. An emigrant told me he could walk four or five hundred miles on dead cattle and, he says, graves are almost without number. Five dollars has been given for a pound of flour. The person above alluded to told me he saw the Meigs County boys at the head of the Humboldt. He remembered the names of Westfall and Comstock.[6] Thirty-six men returning across the plains were all murdered by a gang of French, Spaniards, and Indians. One Californian was reported to have seventy thousand dollars. Careless security proved their ruin; they were murdered in Thousand Spring Valley. We were on the same on the eighth of August 1849. Reeves almost well. The past week very cloudy. This morning a little rain. Winter is coming. Heard Dewing has left North Fork. Wrote two notes to him, neither of which he has received as I heard he knew nothing of where we were. We are anxious to see him. There is not one-half as much sickness this as last fall, owing principally, I think, to the superior quality of food and the general distribution of vegetables throughout the mines.

SEPTEMBER 17: Just returned from Auburn.[7] Found Arm-

strong and Logan, a pleasant meeting after a year's separa-
tion. We found a letter in Auburn written by William Wilson telling where we might find him and the rest of the boys,
but we were just three days too late. He and Asa Condee
have gone home.[8] We felt mad to think we could not even
see them. Little though it might be, we knew it would be a
pleasure to our friends; it would relieve them from the worst
state of mind—suspense. It rained very hard Sunday night
[September 15].

SEPTEMBER 23: Have a very bad cold. For a considerable
time past my mind has been so unsettled that I have lost a
great amount of rest. This, with traveling in the hot sun,
made me feel feverish, which caused me to drink too much
water. My throat and breast are sore. This is the second very
bad cold since I left home. The prospect for digging about
here at present is dull, but those most familiar in this section
think we can make an ounce per day as soon as the wet season commences. We of course wish for rain. But how is it
with those who have claims on the river? O, that is the other
side. Some rivers pay better than others. Yuba has paid
middling well. Wilson and Condee worked in north of North
Fork of it, but many failed. Perhaps nine out of ten who dam
the rivers fail. Some failed last year; then but few dams were
tried and comparatively few failed.

SEPTEMBER 26: I have not been well enough to work yet. A
few minutes since my attention was attracted by a line of
ants; I traced it the whole length which I judge is but very
little less than one-fourth of a mile, averaging from four to
six an inch. In some places their road bends for what reason
I cannot see, but I suppose they have their engineers out and
to them matters appear in a different light. In one place (a

rod or more long), I saw they were as careful to keep in the shade as men would be. I have often noticed them in great numbers.

A RIGHTEOUS VERDICT

Last winter a Dr. Swan, said to be of Illinois, made his home in Auburn. He was famed, if not for skill, certainly for heavy charges. A young man from one of the eastern states employed him. The Doctor had to ride five miles, for which he charged six ounces. His bill in all was nearly four hundred dollars, of which the patient paid two hundred eighty-nine. Some time this summer the Doctor finds him and he has not money to pay. He had been sick nearly all the time, but this is no excuse to the disciple of Aesculapius, he must have every cent. He sues him, a jury of miners is impaneled. After a careful hearing the verdict: The worthy Doctor pays back to the defendant eighty-nine dollars, and also pays the costs of the court, probably fully equal to the remaining two hundred dollars. Swan is now at Johnson's Ranch. Some doctors, however, are very moderate. This class asked two dollars for extracting a tooth, others one-half ounce, or even upwards.

SEPTEMBER 30: This evening Earheart, Graham, Townshend, and Ferrill came from Yuba. Earheart is bound for home. Yuba has proven unfortunate to all except Wilson and Condee. The amount of gold in the stream is amazing, but it is deposited in spots, which is pretty much the same case in all the streams. One in ten may succeed, but not more. Many are leaving those streams in the mountains in consequence of snow. Snow has fallen in sufficient quantities to cause a freshet. At first snow fell, then followed by rain. Many streams raised four feet, sweeping off races and dams. In some instances men were getting two to four dollars per bucket of dirt. How uncertain is mining!

OCTOBER 7: Earheart has gone home. He made some seven to eight hundred dollars; this he made in a short time on Deer Creek. I sent two letters by him. I also sent some specimens, two pieces of gold and a piece of gold and quartz mixed. Stevens of Rutland accompanied him. Our company have generally done pretty well, most of them have a few hundreds. Barnes has gone home with nearly two thousand dollars. Most of us unfortunates will winter in a town C. Giles had the honor of naming.[9] He made a speech on the occasion showing this to be land of Ophir and thought it but fair to name at least one place with the ancient name, so Ophir it is. Giles and I work together this winter as boss boot and shoe-makers. The weather is very dry. Eleven of us that started from Ohio together met here this week. Steadman has been messing with us. H. Dixon has made nothing. Alice Jenkins has poisoned herself so H. Dixon says.

OCTOBER 24: A little rain on Wednesday. At present clear and hot. Earheart and Stevens back, the cholera somewhat alarmed them; this, with the increased rates of passage, determined their course for this winter. Were I to start for home and feel forced to forego that pleasure of a reunion, it would pain me to the quick. The rush homewards is so tremendous every class of vessels is being employed. The liners have nearly doubled their former prices, one hundred fifty dollars is now asked for steerage to Panama.[10] The accomodations are represented as wretched in the extreme. Shepard, one of our company, has gone home with one thousand eight hundred dollars made by cutting hay. He made some three hundred dollars more but lost it by depositing his gold with a firm that have suspended payments. Three others of the company have deposited money in the same house: Graham one thousand one hundred dollars, Rathburn one thousand four hundred, Stevens five hundred. It is very uncertain that they will ever receive a cent.

OCTOBER 21: This week we have been building, our house is nearly finished. It is made of clapboards, fourteen by sixteen feet, a very genteel little edifice. Drake is now working with Steadman. They have done well. This week they made one-half ounce per day. Drake and I have been partners ever since we commenced mining, and we have never quarreled. We part with regret. Here I find I am one day too fast.[11]

OCTOBER 27: Last week spent in going to Cold Spring. My business was to get my clothes and sell our cabin. I found the place wonderfully changed, some fifty or a hundred new houses built. All the faces, with the exception of some one-half dozen, were strange. Those I knew have all done well, making one thousand five hundred dollars and upwards. Places we thought poor have proven very rich. I viewed all our old diggings with a feeling of regret. Our house was occupied, some declaring themselves the veritable owners. I had some difficulty but at last succeeded in getting fifty-five dollars. I witnessed a lawsuit in a tavern whose walls was decorated with lewd pictures, two justices hearing. The case was a plain one, the defendant an Irishman. The prosecuting attorney for Eldorado County happened to be in the room drunk. He cursed the defendant because he was a foreigner. I asked him where he found such a law as that. His constant cry was against foreigners. The Indians in the vicinity of Hangtown and Weavertown are bringing the vengence of the whites on themselves. Some fifteen or twenty persons are missing, and it is believed they are dead. Two hundred men left Coloma on Friday intending to hold the Indians in check until they hear from the Governor. Saw Bowers, he has made some one thousand five hundred dollars, and had eight hundred of it stolen.

NOVEMBER 3: Weather variable, generally cloudy but no rain. The general health pretty good. There is considerable diarrhea, but not as much as this time last year. The cholera is at length in California. It is worse in Sacramento than in San Francisco. The past week the number of deaths in Sacramento was thirty to fifty per day. Those recently arrived and the intemperate fall prey most readily. Some cases are reported in the mines, one at Placerville, or Hangtown, one at Nevada, and one in this place. Those persons were recently in Sacramento. Mail came in but no letter for me.

NOVEMBER 10: Thursday we heard that Dr. Dixon, of St. Louis, was killed by the Indians near Johnson's Ranch, some ten miles from Hangtown. We immediately thought that Hugh Dixon was dead. John Earheart rode over to ascertain the fact. This evening he returned with a sad confirmation of our worse fears. The two brothers are no more, both died violent deaths and their bodies rest near each other.

Hugh fought bravely after receiving a ball through the leg. He was mortally wounded by a ball through the bowels. His body remained in the possession of the Indians for some hours and was desperately mangled. One of his brothers-in-law was near him at the time of his death. Nine fought two hundred. When I was at Cold Spring the week before last I saw him, then healthy and full of hopes, now inanimate dust. Such is life.

NOVEMBER 17: Yesterday I received a letter from home. All well. How great and good is the Author of all things, and O how unmindful are we of His manifold mercies! All the letter was very pleasant, but my brother Robert's part over-powered me with happiness. Beautiful, simple, and from the heart, as a drop of water to the parched lips of a shipwrecked mariner, so is thy letter to me, my brother. The heart is a fountain of many emotions. Who can know its depth?

No rain yet, weather cold with some frost. Last night, as I was making my bed, I could see sparks of electricity. There is quite an effort put forth by the different towns in this county (Sutter) to secure the capital. Ophir (a city a month old) thought it had a fair claim, but we must wait. Last night two temples were dedicated to Bacchus; Pluto might rejoice to hear the noise. Saw several Atheneans or Athenean Mes-sengers. I felt rejoiced to see it, but soon found it the same old thing, an advertisement of a meeting in Albany. I felt very much like being there if I could. The compromise bill passed, slavery triumphant.[12]

NOVEMBER 24: Wednesday it commenced to rain so that all may now get to work. Cholera very bad in the cities of Sacra-mento and San Francisco, deaths variously estimated at forty to one hundred per day. Several have died here in epileptic fits. No doubt the awful shock the nerves receive by working in cold water is mainly the cause. A Mr. Veeder had some forty fits in forty-eight hours, varying from twenty minutes to two hours. No person expected him to recover, but he is now well, except some wildness in his brain. His brain was so ter-ribly excited that he did not sleep until he had taken three tablespoon of laudanum. Dr. Earheart attended.

Our city is a large place with several hundreds of houses, some of the largest made of cloth, a great many of clapboards, but some are built of boards sawed for California use, one edge quite thin. They are four feet long and done up in dozens. They make a very pretty house. Some have large windows, panel doors, and perhaps a glass handle to the lock. We are on Second Street, in Buckeye Row. We have two windows. H. Graham, merchant, is opposite the Giles and Banks Boot Store. Said boot establishment is the second door below Dr. Earheart's, Armstrong and Ferrill, ranchers and horse merchants, a few doors below. All in pretty good health.

DECEMBER 1: A rainy week but the ravines are not running. We have a long run ready for use. It is some seven feet long, straight, except that the end turns up a little. At about half is an open box, the lower half a sheet iron screen, under this a riffle box to catch the gold. This machine saves the labor of one hand and saves the fine gold better than the cradle. I have been somewhat unwell. More cholera in Sacramento. Here many are sick. Dewing, Graham, and Ferrill gone up in the mountains. Dewing made some seven hundred dollars up there.

DECEMBER 8: The prospect seems worse as the season advances. Every ravine is torn up this winter; dirt will be washed the fourth or fifth time. Many have dirt banked up to wash as soon as there is water. Giles went today to Nevada City, some forty miles to see how the land lies in that direction. I am afraid it is like here, all torn up to let the gold out. Wrote home this week.

DECEMBER 15: Cholera has been very fatal in this place the past week, one day three died. A young man of New York city was conversing with a friend of mine in the evening; four hours later he was a corpse. The burying ground is up the side of a bleak mountain, a short distance from and in full view of the town. The dead are now committed to the ground in a coffin; formerly a blanket was his only covering. S. Townshend had a slight attack. Earheart attended him. Giles came home on Friday.

DECEMBER 22: Time wears away but the prospect does not brighten. No water in the ravines, but few making much. Men are forced to be economical; but little is doing in our line. Five shoemakers and not more than work for one. Thursday I saw a shocking spectacle; an unfortunate mortal tired of life cut his throat. He had been sick several weeks and dispair pointed out but one course; three gashes with a large butcher knife and he fell. He appeared not to have strength equal to his resolve. He cut deep in his windpipe, but he left the juglar vein uninjured. Every effort was made to save him but in vain. He died last evening. Conky, but one year since he left Ireland. Character good.

DECEMBER 25: Christmas. Little did I think this day a year ago that I should be in California now. Then bright prospects of home and this time were mingled in my brain. Now next Christmas, and yet peradventure even then denied. How strange is a glance into the future, painted as the mind directs, now clear and beautiful, again dark and uninviting. Everything teaches let reason enlightened by inspiration hold a tight rein, but how hard to submit, how difficult to prevent storm after storm passing over the dark way. I am not happy tonight. Much sickness and many deaths. Not very well.

DECEMBER 29: Weather continues dry. This place is becoming quite deserted, probably not half the population there was one month since. A great many are going to Yuba to work on a flat said to contain a thousand acres paying four to thirty-two dollars per day. Giles went to see it. All claimed.

It is near Marysville, some forty miles from here. I think we will work near here on the river until there is sufficient water in the ravines. Some prophesy no more rain this winter.

It is often surprising how great a matter a little fire kindleth. Christmas evening two drunken men were fighting, one much larger than the other. A man near stopt the unequal fight and probably thought no more of it. Next morning, as he was bent down fixing his door, the larger of the two combatants (an Englishman) shot him, the charge entering just above the right kidney and coming out near the collar bone on the same side. The murderer was hanged in Auburn the next day. He died without the least fear or remorse. The sheriff tried to bring him to some place of security to have him tried by the civil law, but the miners gave him a fair and impartial trial. Twelve men brought in a verdict of guilty. They put a rope around his neck and threw the other end over a limb of a tree. They jerked him fifteen feet in a moment. Another outrage near Auburn, an attempt at robbery and murder.

JANUARY 5, 1851: Another year commenced, another also gone. Regrets are vain and yet who does not regret some portion of the past? Life is a journey we drive but once, and it is necessary to see the contrasts, or all would be blank. Our trials and troubles are our schooling, preparing us for future usefulness. This will be the effect on those who have any spark of latent goodness in them, but some become fiends incarnate. I am now sitting on the banks of North Fork in a tent. It is now raining and Giles is trying to cook. A queer sight; a fire against a rock, a cake baking, but not very fast as the rain puts a veto on the process. Here we make three dollars per day.

JANUARY 12: Left the river last Sunday in the rain. Went to work in the ravine, make two dollars and fifty cents one day, and but very little all week. Water failed, nearly as dry as ever. Drake and Steadman doing well. I know that we prospect too much. No mail yet.

JANUARY 19. Time passing, but no nearer home. Feel almost distracted. This week saw a man whipped for stealing, to the no small delight of many, but some remembered he was a man. Went to see a grizzly. He is some five months old, very docile, and playful. George Reeves making sixteen to twenty dollars per day. Weather like summer. Dewing and company not making much. Ferrill came down.

JANUARY 21: Just read two letters, one from home, the other from Cornelius and Jane. I read them last evening when I received them. Now I have carefully perused their contents, and feel impelled to record my emotions. Every person feels the power of evil sometimes struggling in his heart, but the thoughts these epistles inspire raise my soul to a pure atmosphere. Our spirits are united, and that which cements hearts is holy. How happy I feel. I am in the midst of friends. We think of each other, we live for each other. O how sad, how shipwrecked is he who has lost his home! Few know that magic of the word home. That man is villain who has no home, nor expects one in Heaven; he neither regards man nor fears God.

Tomorrow I leave here for Yuba. None of our company go with me. Giles is prospecting on Bear River. Earheart has been talking with me some time; he will return in a short time. Now I am alone, but not in thought. O what a piece of work is man, and how beautiful are thy ways, O God!

JANUARY 31: The last of January. Sometimes I almost think

it is folly to record my thoughts and, as for my actions, that one word expresses all. Everything seems against me. As the ancients say, the fates are not propitious. My heart aches and my head rings, but all this is folly. I have just returned from Yuba. Nothing for me there. Worked hard one and a half days and made two dollars and fifty cents. When I was going I admired the beauty of this strange land, the wide, grand plain bound by lofty and picturesque mountains, the buttes towering in the North and the snowclad Sierra Nevadas almost forming a semicircle on the East. My step was buoyant and my spirit free. Hope led the way, but coming back my mind was a prey to low and gloomy thoughts. I can settle on scarcely any definite plan of action. Many are going to the Gold Bluffs and Klamath River.[13] Large numbers to Feather. Giles has gone to the former. Earheart has heard that Wilson and Condee are home. Weather delightful, no rain or appearance of it. Not even one fourth the dirt that was thrown up washed. Everything looks miserably discouraging. I can scarcely say "Hope in hope ever." Preserve me O God!

All ravines are called dry diggings, but often no river is more wet. At first the name was appropriate, then gold was picked out of dry dirt. Reeves, Silvester Stephens, and myself are working in a large ravine. We dig eight or nine feet, more than half below water. We have a pump which must be constantly worked, and even then we are frequently in water. Drake is working in a dry ravine and wheels their dirt some fifteen or twenty feet to this ravine. Drake found a lump weighing fifty-six dollars. We have found one weighing twenty-four dollars. The way miners are going north is a sight. Hundreds to Klamath and Scott's rivers (Morrow has gone to Scott's).[14] Vast numbers are going to Feather River, and also up our old track to headwaters of the American. How many hearts now buoyant will be sad next fall?

One young man of Illinois kept tavern. He anticipated a fortune, but found himself involved some three or four hundred dollars. His parents wrote for him to return home; they little knew his situation. His heart failed him and he rushed from time to eternity by his own hand, a bullet pierced his aching heart. All well.

FEBRUARY 9: Worked the past week with Reeves and Green Buler. They have a great deal of dirt that promises to pay well. They offered me four dollars per day and board, but I thought best to buy a share of their dirt. I have agreed to give them one hundred dollars for a third of provisions on hand and an equal share of all proceeds of mining. This week made nearly forty dollars. Today wrote a letter for home. When I reflect on the cause of such vast numbers of men absenting themselves from most of the pleasures of civilized life, that it is all for gold, not gold exactly, but that which it commands, and who can say what it does not make obedient to its will? Monarchs reign by it, men are enslaved for it, men and women marry for it. Yes, more immortal spirits worship thee O Gold. Who knows thy power? What may be the fate of a lump of the precious metal caught by the hands of some rough miner? Let the preceding answer. The bar I was on while at Yuba is named Owesly's Bar. (The bars are named for the first man or company that worked it; there are exceptions—Murderer's, Rattlesnake, Stony, Brushy, Rich, and Condemned.[15]) This bar covers one thousand acres, and a vast number have encamped on it. I was told vermin seem indigenous to the soil and that the proper name is Lousy Bar. This might also be said of other places.

FEBRUARY 20: Dr. Earheart has very kindly offered to carry this home. Should I never return it will be a mournful pleasure to see these pages. If, on the contrary, our Creator returns me to the society of my cherished friends, there is much that will perhaps form a momento for useful conversation. From this time forth I will also continue to note such things as appear important at the time. Earheart is now waiting.

To you my parents and family I give this farewell.

/s/ John Banks

Take care of this for my sake.

Auburn-Ophir

February 23—November 23, 1851

[John Banks remained in the vicinity of Auburn throughout most
of 1851. There he worked placer ground with limited success.
Other, more adventurous, Buckeye Rovers conducted their
searches at higher elevations and, for the most part, accumulated
modest fortunes. Many of Banks's associates returned home in
late November, 1851, but he decided to stay in California for a
time in the hope of finding gold in the diggings at or near Ophir.]

FEBRUARY 23: Sunday, 1851. Yesterday Earheart started for
home, and I sent my journal by him. I perhaps place more
value on it than any others may. I should very much regret
its loss.[1] I have carried it many hundreds of miles. Some rain
the past week, today cloudy. As usual I made but little. Some
are coming back from Feather River, snow there very deep.
Snow now within a few miles of this place.

MARCH 2: Sunday. A little rain but not enough to wash dirt
in the ravine. Made about fifty cents per day and worked constantly. Reports are very favorable from Klamath and Fall
Rivers. A twelve pound lump of gold is shown in Sacramento,
said to have been found on Scott River. The same lump was
exhibited as a specimen of the southern mines. Thousands
live by excitement, and the last discovery is always the richest.

Many of those that went to Scott River are reported to be in great distress. Snow has fallen ten feet deep in the mountains. Relief trains have gone out. Packing into the Scott River costs four dollars per one hundred pounds, mules four hundred dollars per head.

MARCH 9. Sunday. Last week a German died of consumption near us. I think he was but poorly attended. I had seen him out gathering chips, apparently unable to stand. Last winter he went into a gambling house in Sacramento. He had fastened his mule outside. Someone told him his mule was stolen. He left on the table three thousand dollars, which was speedily removed to more careful pockets. He lost both money and mule. He was known here by the name of Monte. His body lies within a few feet of his house. Some Germans put a cross on his head. My bargain with Reeves will not make me rich. Reeves and Stevens have gone out prospecting. Some twenty have agreed to bear their expenses. They will have a hard tramp. This day I received two letters, one from home, the other from Sister Jane. News good.

MARCH 16: Sunday. Tomorrow we start for the mountains, a very hard and doubtful trip. Last spring I had a mule. This time I must do my own packing. I hope the results may be different in the fall. Isaac Dewing and Steadman have started for Feather River. Reeves found nothing encouraging. They saw Harvey Graham some seventy miles up. His health was good, and he was making eight to ten dollars per day. This evening I went with a letter for home to a Dr. Scott. He is going to Ohio. I saw some of the boys on a spree. They were yelling and whooping, the subject for a good temperance lecture. Made thirty-seven dollars in five weeks, a poor speculation. The weather is most delightful.

MARCH 23: Nevada City. Cold and just clearing after a very severe storm—rain, snow and wind. This has been the most severe spell of bad weather this winter. A strange finale to a very mild winter. About this time last spring we were on our journey up this mountain and experienced just such weather. We got into a house at twenty dollars per month—eleven of us. Provisions: flour ten dollars a hundred pounds, pork twenty-five dollars a hundred pounds. Times rather dull. Wages five dollars a day.

The Coyote Diggings are astonishing to view.[2] Some shafts are sixty to seventy feet deep. Whole hills have been torn so that the surface is falling in. Most of the leads are dug so that they meet, causing a circulating of air. Many have sheds over the shafts, so that they may work even in the rain. Two men raise the bucket by means of a windlass.

Last year there was but little water, two or three barrels perhaps in twenty-four hours; and with that little amount miners washed dirt. North Rock and Deer creeks are conveyed in ditches to the tops of the hills. The ditches are Deer and Eight Miles Rock.[3] Since the water has been brought in, miners find it difficult to bail their leads. Water is sold at one to eight dollars per day, sufficient to run a Long Tom. Very large fortunes have been made in this place. Last week there was a very destructive fire in this place. The best portion of the town is destroyed. The loss is variously estimated at two hundred fifty to over six hundred dollars. Such is the rapidity of things here that several large houses are already up, and in a few days all will be replaced. Yet this, like some other places, is overgrown. Many houses are for sale or rent in suburbs of this city in the mountains. Grass Valley, where we spent two nights, is quite a town. Its principal machine is in operation, and two more are about to be started.[4] Twelve mortars are worked by steam. Three men attend it. Quartz is forty dollars per ton.

MARCH 30: Almost constant storm—rain, hail, and snow. Wild stormy March, the worst month in the year. Worked twelve days at five dollars per day. The diggings in this place are in the hands of a few men. Laws: A man may hold all he buys; fifty men may hold claims in as many places and work in but one; and further, as tools are often stolen, no tools are required to be left. In all other places, they are considered the only evidence of possession. Sometimes I think of staying in this region, but working by the day I won't do. This evening twenty-five hundred dollars was stolen from a banker. A thousand dollars reward. If caught, the thief must hang. A circus has been in operation the last week. Paid one dollar for a box for two. For the first few days a thousand attended. Sundays they exhibit twice. As in the West, a large tent is the place of display. This evening bought an anti-slavery paper of Salem, Ohio, the first of that class I have seen in California. A letter from Sibley and an able speech of Phillips at Lynn, Massachusetts, are its principal articles.[5] It reminds me much of old times. Health good.

APRIL 3: Very wet, almost constant heavy showers. The robbers that robbed Mr. Napper of his money have been tried by lynch law. The people thought the civil authorities might let them slip by. The tribunal, judge and jury, behaved in a dignified manner, but the mob was very indecent. Shouting, cursing, laughing, and lewd obscenity marked the conduct of many. The prisoners—Allen of Brown County, Ohio; Rigsby of Terre Haute, Indiana; and Miller [blank]—at first stoutly denied all knowledge of the theft; but as the evidence poured in, Allen thought best to confess. Perhaps a more worthy motive induced him. Rigsby and Miller took a solemn oath of innocence. Rigsby said: "The last words I shall utter on the scaffold are 'I am innocent.'" Mr. Ellis, counsel for the prisoners, made an eloquent defense and solemnly protested against the whole proceedings. He promised the prisoners life if they would confess. The jury brought in a verdict of guilty in Allen and Miller's case—sentence to receive twenty lashes on the bare back; and if Miller did not tell where his share of the money was, nineteen additional lashes. This brought him to terms. He said he had eight hundred dollars hidden at Rough and Ready Diggings, ten miles off.[6] In the meantime, Rigsby was again tried. Now two were against him and a fair probability of hanging. He also confessed. But as he was Napper's clerk and enticed the others, he received a sentence of thirty-nine lashes.

Last night, surrounded by thousands, they were whipped. Allen, who was a captain in the army in Mexico, scarcely flinched. Rigsby and Miller begged most piteously. Rigsby screamed and groaned so that I was unwilling to see more. Their sentence was that if they stayed in town tonight, they should be hanged. Allen left, but the others were very sick. Rigsby, it is thought, must die. His character was almost unimpeachable. A wife and five children must bear a sad tale. Rigsby begged to be hanged. Boys and worthless men would have yelled and insulted them admidst their groans but for a few resolute men. The whip is very heavy and bruised rather than cut. Rigsby's back was black and bleeding. I saw Allen's back—the blood was oozing from every stroke. All he said to the executioner was, "A little higher up." The Dutchman who flogged them was well pleased with his job.

On Monday we found a place to work which, according to law and justice, we have every right to have. Today five men say they will work it, that they bought it. Others say they bought it. All proving each to be a liar, yet such claims a general rule here. All combine to cheat those that want employment. There is more monopoly in claims here than in any other place in California that I have seen or heard of. As usual nothing very flattering. The weather is very unhealthy. One or two deaths a day. The graveyard is large and looks more like a country burying ground than anything I have seen. Many of the graves are enclosed by paling and some have neat boards at their head. Two graves have a house built over them so that no stranger may disturb their resting place. The number is over one hundred.

APRIL 5: Sunday. Weather yet unfavorable. Erysipelas is bringing many to the tomb. Snow very deep in the mountains, fourteen feet at Onion Valley on Feather River.[7] Fifty thousand are said to have gone up. Mules and horses in great number are lying dead at the upper end of the journey. Many are doubtless suffering. Some are reported frozen. One month since there was scarcely any snow in that region, and no one dreamt of such weather at this season. I have become acquainted with a Dr. Enscoe, Fellow of Trinity College, Dublin, the son of a Separatist. He knew several my father knew—Walker, Morgan, Mansel and others.[8] Though he was not a member and was but little among them since he was thirteen years old, it awakened an old chord that afforded pleasure.

He obtained his degree in Edinburgh and has been many years in Belgium.

APRIL 9: Thursday. This day two years from home. Now no better off than then and much older. I am now two miles south of Grass Valley going back to Ophir. Bad as we thought it, it is perhaps best. Eighteen months past we slept near this place. What would our spirits have been had we known the future and could see no way of avoiding the present result?

APRIL 12: Sunday. Ophir. Reached here Friday evening. Traveled nearly thirty miles with bedding and clothes weighing some thirty pounds. Found two letters for me, news from the beginning of February. All well. Barnes and Shepard are home. As far as I can learn, those who return are generally believed to possess more gold than they have. Human beings are subject to inflations. "What lacks in matter is made up in wind." Cornelius gives a lecture on Fowlerism.[9] Phrenology run *mad*. Fourierism cannot bring the millenium forward as fast as Fowlerism.[10] Examine the young one's bumps and if bad, kill him. By this sorting out process the world might soon produce a good crop. The Spartans were nearer right than 2,000 years of light and knowledge finds us. Oh what an expressive word is humbug: knockers [in seances], fortune tellers, money getters. Acquisitiveness is at large.

Madame Rumor said there were piles of gold in the northern mines. She also stated that not less than 100,000 are up in the snows. Truth says many are starving. We saw Meigs County men who are just down from the mountains. Hunger forced them out. They traveled on snow fifteen feet deep. Some report board is eight dollars per day. Here weather is very warm.

APRIL 19: Sunday. Weather very fine. Here when it rains it is winter even if April and summer in a clear day in January. Made thirty dollars this week. Very few men here at present. Most are at present employed in ravines to which water has been conveyed in ditches. We are using water brought some mile and one half. We are working lower down than the owners after they have used it. Dick Whittington and his cat might enact the old game over again here.[11] I have seen but one cat in California and that was in Coloma one evening this past week. I saw three mice caught by a dead fall at one time and nearly a dozen in the day. It is said rats are stoutly disputing the possession of Sacramento with the Anglo Saxons.

APRIL 26: Sunday. Thought last Sunday I would defer writing until today, thinking it would go by the same mail, but find I was in error. I have lost two weeks, which I regret as I know folks at home are anxious to hear from me. When I wrote last I said I intended going up in the mountain the next day. Next Sunday I must write without fail. Today we had a dividend of the last two weeks, eighty dollars. The best for more than a year. Worked very hard. Worked over the same ground that the famous sixteen pounder was found in. Our largest was $6.50. Weather warm. Health good.

MAY 4: Sunday. I have again to acknowledge the receipt of letters. Though I heard but recently, I was very anxious. News with one exception good. The way of transgressors is hard. [Proverbs, XIII,15] Cousin John's daughter Hannah, an intelligent girl, married John Graves of Zanesville. They were like gay boats on a swift current without a helm. They have dashed themselves headlong against the rocks. What a short race, to die of their own hands in a lonely wood, and to lie for weeks so near the former home of the venerated Adams in the woods at Braintree.[12] Wrote today to Cornelius.

There is some talk of bringing the waters of Bear River to Auburn and vicinity. Here at present but few men, and some of these talk of leaving shortly. Weather most delightful.

MAY 13. Tuesday. Worked hard all day Sunday. Could get the water no other day. Worked Saturday night, also last night, and will this night. We are sluicing in a flat. Saturday night and Sunday we made thirty-six dollars. Dividend for the last two weeks sixty-two dollars. I never believed it criminal to labor on the first of the week if it were nothing could justify but felt I was not acting exactly right. Circumstances forced me and these must palliate. Feel very weary. Arms ache. Weather cool, not very favorable for the early melting of the snow. The great fire in San Francisco destroying three-fourths of the city has afforded merchants an excuse to raise the price of goods, some articles twenty-five per cent.[13] Last Sunday there were three or four fights in town. Some men act as if the sum total of human felicity was to drink, gamble and fight.

MAY 18: Sunday. A most infamous outrage was perpetrated in this place last Thursday afternoon. Six Indians, accompanied by a squaw wife of one of them, came into town. Those gamblers that have been keeping this place in excitement some time past were drinking. They sought to make the Indians drunk so that the squaw might be left unprotected. They took hold of their victim. She resisted, and her husband not being as drunk as was thought rushed to her rescue. Though in the midst of vindictive and powerful enemies without one ray of hope, he asserted his noble manhood, and the husband rose superior to fear. He drew his knife and rushed at them. The others kept aloof. The unfortunate man was instantly felled by a club to the groin, and his skull was fractured. He has since died. Worthless Indian, noble white man. His murderer's name is Anderson, formerly a Georgian slave driver, strange to say, not void of some good qualities. This transaction caused no murmurs. I heard nothing of it until evening.

MAY 25: Sunday. Weather cool and pleasant with occasional clouds. Worked five nights this past week, Monday and Tuesday nights until two or three o'clock, the others about midnight. We were sluicing. Made fifty-six dollars in all.

Ours is a ground sluice very much the same as a small ravine. There is no way superior to this to save gold, where there is sufficient water and fall enough to carry off what we term tailings or washed earth. We worked on a flat. There are some hundreds of acres of ground in the vicinity of Auburn that with a sufficiency of water would in this way pay four to ten dollars per day.

A contractor had taken the job of bringing waters of Bear River here in sixty days in a ditch nine feet wide at the top, three feet wide at bottom and four feet deep, distance twenty-five miles. Provisions falling in price, flour nine cents, butter sixty cents, ham twenty-two, etc.

Feel very tired and weary. Washed gold out of a sluice today that we worked in seven days (all time spent) and got but four dollars for pay. That certainly will not *pay*. While speaking of phrases I think of one I heard a day or two since. "What news from *Sydney*?" an ominous question.[14] Cants borrowed from the card table or ball alley are quite fashionable. If you do remarkably well mining, some will say "he made a strike." From recent news it appears but few if indeed

any intend crossing the plains this season. The road will present monuments of last summer's suffering for years to come.
Report says thirteen men were recently murdered by Indians
not very far from Hangtown. They had just started for home
across the plains. One is said to be the mail carrier from
here to Salt Lake.

JUNE 1: Sunday. Got up at daybreak and went to work.
Forced to quit about eleven o'clock on account of a shortage
of water. This is almost as hard a plan as staying up in the
first part of the night. We take a piece of bread and eat
nothing more until noon. I think I never heard anything
equal to the melody of song poured forth at the dawn. It
would seem as if their joy knew no bounds as they see the
sun rise. Gratitude for another day is sent forth in rapturous
bursts of delight The lark and mockingbirds are foremost.
Made but twenty-one dollars this week. Today is brother William's birthday. Twenty-six years old, but his birth seems
but the other day. Feel very tired, a hard way to work.

JUNE 8: Sunday. Received a letter from home written April
first. All well. Wrote home today. Last week I made forty-two
dollars. When I was going to Nevada City I saw a number of
Chinese encamped on Bear River.[15] They are very sociable. I
took tea with them and of course saw them handle their chopsticks. It is astonishing what a large quantity they can force
into their mouths. Rice seems a favorite dish and well displays
the accomplishments of chopsticking. There are a large number of them working near us. I saw one of them a day or two
since carrying a heavy load balanced on a pole. He walked
along nicely, adjusting his load on his shoulder with one hand
and carrying an umbrella to shade the sun with the other.

They strongly resemble the Indian. When I heard a lot of them ridicule a young fellow who went to Auburn and rigged himself in new pants, hat, silk vest, and sash, "Indian, Indian," they said. I thought that is rather too true to make a joke of. I believe they are very inoffensive and a few are quite intelligent. It seems they must differ in everything from the balance of mankind. The Frenchman, the Spaniard, and the American can play cards together; but here the man with the chopsticks is decidedly out. He must have more than twice as many cards, and queer articles they are. Chinese dislike the Indians. Made forty-one dollars last week.

JUNE 14: Saturday. Although there is no slavery allowed here by law, yet there is one of the most infamous kinds in the world. Women of abandoned morals are brought here and sold to the highest bidder. Their sale price is received by enterprising ship captains. There is a house being fitted up in town in a very gaudy manner for the reception of this kind of women. This worthy keeps the house where the Indian was killed. There is a great deal of drunkenness and fighting. Many men seem to work just enough to buy liquor. I think of this class a large majority are from the South. Most of the Southerners are of the non-driving fraternity. Jolly fellows.

JUNE 15: Sunday. The scene of Sodom was almost reenacted here last night. Two of that wretched class of women came here last evening and created great excitement. One man was felled with a club and two stabbed with a knife. Today it was reported none were fatally injured. Weather cool with frequent clouds. Yesterday worked by myself, partner sick. Made $20.50. All week made but a little over thirty dollars. E. Armstrong and Ferrill have gone to Feather River. Some are reported to be doing very well there. Owens of Wilks makes three or four ounces per day. None of the other boys are making much. Some near here are reported to be making $50 per day. As in all the mines, a few are doubtless doing well.

JUNE 22: Sunday. Much better luck this week than usual. Made $135. We took nearly all of that out in two days. One day I picked up forty-nine dollars in my hand at one time, one piece weighing $25.50. Next day, Wednesday, I dug a fifty-five-dollar piece. I should and do feel grateful for such good fortune. Reeves and company could make nothing here and have this day started for Nelson Creek.[16] H. Graham is reported to have a claim worth $20,000. A big story, but these are the tales that draw men after them. Weather warm. Most of the time there is a cool breeze from the land at night and the sea in the day. Hear of no sickness. Received a most excellent letter from home.

JUNE 29: Sunday. Weather very warm. Yesterday the mercury rose to 128 degrees Farenheit in the sun. If it were not for a constant breeze it would be impossible to work. We go to work at six and quit one-half past eleven or twelve. Go to work at two and work until nearly sundown. Today I wrote a letter for John Leahy. He made over $2,000 in a year. He has been in America six years. He sent for a brother and three children. He is going to send for his sister and one child. He has also sent $50 per year to his father. He now intends to have his family settle around him somewhere in the West. He is a common, coarse-looking Irishman, but has a pair of fine eyes. His brother's family are in Providence, Rhode Island. Made twenty-one dollars.

JULY 6: Sunday. I am now thirty-three years of age and I may say I am thankful not married yet. This seems to be the great end and aim of man's life—to hunt for something almost angelic, and I suppose he must find at last that they are something like himself, pretty *hard cases.* Oh, you sour old bachelor! On the evening of the Fourth we had a very handsome balloon made of paper let off from our city. It was twenty-one feet long. I spent that day in a way I regret, waiting about town for the ascension. Drunkenness was the order of the day.

JULY 13: Sunday. Gold digging is certainly a strange business. G. Reeves sunk a hole within a few feet and some other persons not more than one foot of a five-ounce piece we found on Friday. Many have often tried to find a lead in that part of the ravine. We resolved to dig a ditch through it. For this purpose we took two men into our company: both of Pomeroy, Ohio, Price and Thompson. Very few are working near us. Men hold large claims in these mines. Last year there were fifteen on the big ravines, twenty-five on its tributaries. Now there are sixty and seventy-five, respectively.

The Legislature declares all laws made by miners regulating claims legal. Article two states tools must be on the claim. They are the only evidence of possession. The claim must be worked at least one in every five days, except the owner is sick; and all dirt thrown up in dry ravines may be held. Article three: Water must not be thrown out of its original channel to the injury of miners on that stream. Article four: No man can hold more than one claim by any pretext whatever. Article five: All difficulties must be settled by referees.

Our neighborhood has been very quiet lately. I hear of several murders at a distance, one only nine miles off. The victim was killed for forty dollars. The Indian Anderson was thought to have killed has recovered. Almost every day we see men breaking quartz hunting for a rich vein. Weather very cool.

JULY 20: Sunday. Weather excessively hot. Made nothing this week. We find it a very difficult task to find the original channel. Heard from the boys in the mountains. This hot weather is a most delightful time for fleas. In Drake and Reeves' house they jump to meet every person who comes in. If they but understood the grand secret of human power through combination, they might move the house at one bound. I saw the owl today having an awfully wise countenance. His eyes were very cadaverous. His large whiskers and full chin gave him quite a patriotic cast of countenance.

JULY 23: Wednesday. Paid six dollars for drawing two teeth. I have never felt such pain as I suffered last night. They have plagued me a long time but last night doomed them. The job is well done.

JULY 27: Sunday. Brother James' birthday. I had some expectation of a letter today, but the mail is very large, the largest ever sent to California. The news by the paper is not very important. The old game of president-making seems to be in a thriving state, judging by the number of names talked of. We are not making anything. Our ditch business is unlucky so far. Weather fine.

AUGUST 3: Sunday. Heat excessive. Made nothing this week, though we dug some 200 feet of the ravine. Our ditch is three to five feet deep, eighteen inches to two feet wide. The gold lies in spots. Received no letter this week. There is great confusion among the express riders. Most of them are giving up the business. Miners move so much that many letters are left as dead. Besides, the Post Office Department is making some changes. Heard that a post office is open at Auburn. Feel very anxious to hear from home. Read the twentieth chapter of Acts. Paul's farewell is exceedingly touching and beautiful 1,800 years after it was written. "What is man that thou art mindful of him." [Psalms VIII:4.]

AUGUST 10: Sunday. Wrote home today. It appears strange I should feel uneasy, but we are prone to fear the worst. Though I have heard from home monthly during the greater part of the past year, it seems a long time since the last letter. Made thirty-one dollars this week.

AUGUST 17: Sunday. Weather cool and cloudy. Nights quite cold. A good time to work. Dug one pit nine by ten, and nine feet deep. Made but twenty-two dollars in all. Sank another pit almost to the bottom but as yet no prospect of gold. Men are beginning to hunt for winter diggings. Many are taking claims and recording them. Laws in the Auburn District require twenty-five cents to record a claim and it must be worked ten days after the water comes.

AUGUST 24: Sunday. Made scarcely anything this week. Saw Bartlett, an acquaintance just returned from the mountains. He had been running after mammoth stories all summer. He has lost $800 in prospecting within the last year. I know a young man who stood very fair as an honest man, who by a few small dirty tricks has not made one cent, but has lost that which should be dear as life—character. A matter of great importance, viewed in any light you will among miners. There has been another great excitement in Sacramento. Three men were hanged for robbing a man of $200. Two of them being of Sydney hurried them to the scaffold.

AUGUST 31: Sunday. Perhaps there is no place on earth at the present time containing so much active vice flowing along with an equal amount of energetic virtue. Today I saw a handsome young woman engaged at the card table, drinking, gambling, and swearing. Depravity has not had time to demolish all appearance of amiability. Last year she crossed the plains enjoying the respect and esteem of friends and acquaintances. Very many of these unhappy creatures are kept in gambling houses as *bait*. On the other hand, who knows the thousands of men who are enduring toil and every kind of privation for wife and family. How many too of that despised race said to be incapable of any generous or noble exertion are here struggling for Freedom, not merely for themselves but for those for whom they are willing to risk their lives. Friday an aged man of color sat on the bank near where we were working. His dignity of appearance and also evidence of being unwell interested me. I asked what brought him to California. "Five years ago, at the death of my master, I bought my freedom at $350. I now own eighty acres of land and might live comfortably if my family were free. Have a wife and six children in slavery. Could buy my wife and one or two children but not six. How to make the choice? I could not. Their mistress said all shall be yours for $3,000. So here I am, and hope God will give me luck. Only this sickness excepted, I have done well in the mines." Received an exceedingly welcome letter from home. All well but no mention of William Booth.

SEPTEMBER 5: Friday. First wet day this season. Last night quite wet. Miners on the river are viewing this in dread. Some are daily taking out thousands. This is especially the case low down on the streams. One company on the American River take out $1,000 to $3,000 per day. The company next above have a steam engine. Very rich diggings have been discovered up in the mountains near where I spent last summer a year since. At Shirt Tail Canyon, ten miles from Bird's Coyote, diggings yield from nine to twelve ounces to the pan. Accidentally found by the upturning of a tree, a little like the story of the mines of Potosi.[17] Todd's Valley, where we slept a week ago, pays three to four dollars per pan.[18] They are bringing water sixteen miles. This is part of the region Reeves and Stevens prospected in last spring.

Wednesday was the day of election, or one of our grand festivals to Bacchus: Whigs and Democrats fighting as usual. Here the grand principle they are contending for is undeniably *Gold*. The first year delicate-fingered men might be very often seen with pick and shovel in hand working merrily. Times have changed. Can't make one to three or four ounces per day. Shan't blister my hands for four dollars. But now they have discovered the dear people are in a bad *fix*, and Democrat or Whig is equally willing to haul them out if well paid. I did not vote.

Saw Mr. Veazey, one of Giles' company on the trip to Klamath. He made $800, Giles $500, the difference being loss of time prospecting. They left on account of Indians. There the natives are a fierce, manly, warlike set of fellows. Near Giles' camp a Mr. Blackburn kept a trading post. His house was built of clapboards. The Indians resolved to plunder and destroy this place. Five men encamped near there were murdered in their beds. Blackburn heard the noise and awakened his wife. He had two rifles in readiness. The Indians immediately made the attack. The night was dark, but Blackburn fired by the noise, his wife loading. Four Indians rushed toward the house with torches in hand to fire it, but each fellow carried death in his hand, the light making a sure aim. Day began to dawn, and Blackburn singled out their chief. This ended the fight. The squaws were seated on the bluff above the scene of carnage, baskets in hand to carry off the spoils. Fourteen Indians were killed. This was not the end of the tragedy for Blackburn. A packer told him a man was lying dead in the road a short distance back and ought to be buried. They went to perform this last, sad office for the stranger, as they supposed. But judge Blackburn's horror when he found his father covered with *gore*. The unfortunate old man had left one of the southern valleys to visit his son. This is surely a sad but true picture.

In one region the Indians were shot like wolves. This was on Salmon River.

SEPTEMBER 7: Sunday. Sometimes I feel exceedingly lonesome. When the prospect of a speedy reunion with friends is bright, my spirits are elated. I can bear the present storm, for the haven is near. But when I see that I have almost lost the track and feel the storm of conflicting thoughts rage, my strength seems at times almost ready to fail.

SEPTEMBER 14: Sunday. Saw several of our boys from the mountains. A large number have done well. Drake and Steadman have made some $1,500 each. William Logan has $2,300. Several others have $1,000 each.

Four have gone home with $800 to $1,500. Reeves has not made much. Buler has $1,000.[19] He has gone to a farm his uncle gave him forty miles south of Sacramento.

How hard it is to know what is best here. I have cleared over $400. The last two months made nothing yet worked very hard. In the spring I was in debt and felt I could risk time no longer. I wanted something certain. Now I wish I had gone to the mountains, yet all may be for the best. Mining requires either great hope or recklessness. The former failed me since the first summer, the latter I hope to be forever preserved from.

SEPTEMBER 21: Sunday. Weather fine. The past has been a week of crime. Anderson on Tuesday stabbed and frightfully cut two men, one of whom died of his wounds. The first, a German, he struck with his Bowie knife twice on the head. He then caught him by the head and drew his knife desperately two or three times across his neck, but in his haste he mistook the back for the cutting edge. In an instant he made an effort to use the edge, but the bystanders jumped in and ended it. In the afternoon Anderson was drinking with an elderly man. They seemed hail fellow until they began to talk of what is termed *manhood*. The old man said, "I can whip you." "That's a lie." The old man struck him. Anderson drew his knife, struck the unfortunate wretch on the head. He tried to get under the table. Anderson stabbed him in the calf of the leg, inflicting a desperate wound. He then struck him in the left hip, penetrating the cavity of the abdomen. The unhappy mortal, unable to rise, uttered the most horrible blasphemies, calling for a pistol. His wounds were dressed and he was carried to a house near. He died on Thursday. I was present at the inquest. A party started for Anderson, but he was wise enough to take advantage of the time given him and left. If he had been caught he would have been hanged. Anderson was since in Coloma. I might relate an equally horrible tale of a man found dead in his tent near Auburn. Each of these was in a tavern.

SEPTEMBER 28: Sunday. This seems to be a time of general relaxation. There is but little water. For my part, I have lost but one day this season and that the Fourth of July. This place is middling quiet. But on Horseshoe Bar, on the American River, some five miles from here, two men were killed today, one accidentally.[20] The other was shot by a brother gambler. I have seen several tarantulas, said to be more poisonous than the rattlesnake. They are large spiders covered with hair like a mouse. I killed a large one lately. I have been throwing up dirt in a ravine and a lonely place. I am often pleased to see our quails, a most beautiful bird. The male has an elegant topknot hanging gracefully forward. They don't speak the same language that quails do in Ohio.

OCTOBER 5: Sunday. Lately I received two most excellent letters. That from home is very good. I was grieved to hear that Maria had been sick. Cornelius shows a mind capable of investigating the recesses of the human heart. Weather as bland and as mild as June. A great many are going home.

OCTOBER 12: Sunday. Weather fair. Throwing up dirt yet. Partner working on the north ravine made a few dollars, not much more than board. News from Cuba very melancholy.[21] Poor mortals, what could they expect other than they have received? A descent on a friendly nation the filibusters may name it as they please, but it looks very much like piracy.

OCTOBER 19: Sunday. A good many of our boys have come down from the mountains. Reports rather exaggerated at first, yet most have done well. Wrote a letter to Cornelius but a little too late. I thought it might be in time if it left here Monday, but missed the ship. Got a claim on the big ravine. We made an ounce each one day and but $2.50 yesterday.

OCTOBER 26: Sunday. Yesterday I received a letter from home dated September 6. Another reunion with friends, a fanning of a living fire. A good messenger. Some say you should not reflect on the past. If you make a mistake, forget it and push forward. This seems to sound well enough, but can we? What is life but memory and too often but a bundle of mistakes. I can without the aid of a microscope see many since I left home. But take one of them away, and the chain of life is broken so that even our errors become dear. All animated nature lives in memory. The little wanderer from sunny clime returns to its parents' nest. Man feels its impulse and turns his dying eyes towards the home of his youth. Amidst the erring hours of the wanderer, how often will the memory of mother, home, and friends burst in like lightning in a dark night, warning him of his danger on that desperate road. He closes his eyes though he wishes for light. This but reminds him of the sun gone down. Oh, what is memory to the murderer if his friends are constantly admonishing him of his crime? "Memory by Heaven designed is the loveliest faculty of the human mind."

NOVEMBER 2: The march of civilization is most surely onward. Today we had a grizzly fighting a bull. Some five or six hundred assembled, giving two dollars for the right, but it was a farce. Neither bull nor bear seemed to have any regard for the wishes of human lovers of fun. They were chained together and ropes attached to each. By these ropes they were pulled atop of each other, otherwise the length of the chain would be their nearest point. Some two hours were spent pulling and hauling. Occasionally the bear would hug and bite. The poor bull stood still. At the end of the exhibition the grizzly gave up and the bull gored him a little. The bear might weigh 1,000 pounds.

Reeves came down from the mountains last evening. Armstrong, Ferrill and H. Graham not yet. Heard our claim on the North Fork of Middle Fork paid well this season.

NOVEMBER 9: Sunday. Yesterday rain began to fall. Today cloudy but not much rain. Today we bought a ditch over a mile long taking water to small ravines. Cost $150. If this should prove a dry winter it will be a great benefit as the ravine we take water from is seldom without a considerable stream. Graham, Armstrong and Ferrill are near us. All the Buckeyes in California near here must meet at least one a year. Some have done very well. I wrote home today.

We laid in some provisions. Two hundred pounds of flour at nine dollars a hundred weight. Ham thirty cents a pound. Potatoes, a hundred pounds at eight and a half cents. Thirty-five pounds of butter at fifty-five cents. Tomorrow a Mr. Stearns starts for Ohio. He takes his brother's body with him. The deceased died at the age of forty-nine years. He is encased in lead. The flesh is not much decayed.

NOVEMBER 16: Sunday. A most awful outrage was perpetrated here last Thursday evening. Thomas Hogan of Pittsburgh and Gus Jones of Georgia, two infamous characters, got on a spree and went from tavern to tavern breaking glasses and other property. When remonstrated with in the most calm manner, Hogan and Jones became fiendish with rage, threatening destruction to every person. A Mr. Fuquay, owner of the Union Hotel, ordered them out of his house. They left but returned armed. Jones said to Hogan, you open the ball, and I will close it. He drew his pistol. Fuquay was prepared with a double-barreled gun. At the first fire, Fuquay blew the top of Hogan's skull off. Jones ran, but as he was running received two shots in the hips. Fuquay has been tried and acquitted. Jones will recover.

Some time since I saw crime must be on the increase, but it is most fearfully arrived. Seventeen dead bodies were recently found lassoed near Marysville. Mexicans are accused of the crime, but other men can throw the lasso. The Sacramento paper says seven men were found in the same situation near Auburn. But Auburn is only two miles from here and I heard nothing of it. The result of all this is the formation of vigilance committees. But the end is not yet. Idlers are very numerous in each gambling saloon. Dozens may be seen whose only employment is cheating. They are all well-dressed and apparently full of funds. Within the last three months some six large drinking and gambling saloons have been built. Notwithstanding, the number of miners is not what it was last fall.

NOVEMBER 23: Some rain the past week but only sufficient to cool the atmosphere. At present cloudy. The last week we spent in extending our ditch. It is now nearly two miles long. William Logan came down this week. He is bound for home. He has been very lucky. Four others go with him. In a few days the majority of our company will have bid farewell to mining. Of those here, two are near me, Armstrong and Ferrill. Reeves is at Gold Hill, some four miles down the creek. Townsend has gone to the Secret Diggings, about the same distance.[22] Today I learned the mail has been lost between Havana and Chagres. Two steamers have come since with mail. They brought newspapers but no letters. This will be a sad disappointment.

Logan starts in the morning and I send this with him. My health is good, and as I have said I think I have a reasonable prospect of five or six hundred dollars this winter and spring. My mind is comparatively calm. The haven seems near and my journey nearly drawn to a close.

My errors have been the result of over anxiety in some cases. Other times I might have ventured farther, but hundreds in too ardent a search for gold have lost their lives. Every graveyard attests this. You see in some of my letters something like an effort to exculpate my conduct. Here I confess I am very sensitive. I have reason to think some have falsely represented my actions. At least I have been told so. Some I blame, for others my only feeling is contemptuous pity. Why tell what would wound the hearts of friends? Where I could not answer, I defy anyone to say aught in truth that I will not answer. You from motives I fully appreciate have said nothing of this. But I have seen a little dark eyed malice and foul mistrust, and further some things have been told. Even here I see the weakness of mankind. "As you fall I rise," but friends you should remember that falls hurt. The quarrels of our company are family quarrels. I feel friendship for all but would scarcely expect justice from all. Prejudice of an older date than California had germinated in the breasts of two or three. The other day I heard a little of the contents of two or three letters from a source that in itself is contemptible. A thousand times as much told here would but provoke a smile, but coming this far, I was out of a laughing mood.

Goodbye. If I did not soon expect to see you, I might attempt a further description of this remarkable part of the world. Some of the views are surpassingly grand. Every day when I go to work I look down in the valley which looks almost like a vast lake surrounded by lofty mountains. Here in what is termed the foothills there is an alternate succession of hills and valleys. The appearance of the country is that of one long cultivated land, but for some years lying in a wild state. Bushes in clusters are the only underwood. The Indians have left but little more evidence than the cattle that feed on its bosom. A kind of moat thrown up in a circle resembling a course used by circus actors shows where the Red Man held his wise councils or rejoiced in wild revelry in his council house. Around this are a few mounds where the bark huts stood. But the relic that will last longest in time is their mortars in the rocks. They may be seen almost everywhere. Here the Indian women have worked in a way but few would credit. Here the lover viewed with pride the muscular object of his choice, and she to gain his favor worked like vengeance. He, like our polished dandy, was seeking a fortune, but that fortune lay in his lady's ability to crack acorns.

On every hand I see evidence of volcanic power. The ancient granite is burst up like bubbles in a boiling pot. Not very far from here is a volcano in constant action. Last Friday I picked up a piece of quartz having brimstone in a little cell. I eat off it. The face of the country indicates vast changes. Beds of rivers are found hundreds of feet above their present level. I see places where ancient lakes have burst their barriers. Here the stately buckeye of Ohio has degenerated into a mere bush. The black walnut may be tramped down by an ox. Yet vegetation is powerfully active. From the tall pine to the rich pastures, nature puts forth her power. Her climate is one of the most salubrious in the world. Where could men expose themselves as they do here with like impunity, working in water and bivouacing on the ground? The heat is sometimes excessive, but the sky is clear. This summer the mercury rose to 128 degrees F. in the shade. Throughout September it ranged about 85 degrees F. I would think that at no time this fall has it been as low as 40 degrees F. The winter of 1849 must have been an exception. At present the earth is not wet a foot deep. Here is a wide field for the geologist and the mineralogist. Even the animals, birds and beasts look strange. From the stately deer to the kangaroo rat, they are objects of strange interest.

Bounded by the vast Pacific on one side, here the newest, on otherwise the oldest land. Here also the different tribes of men meet. The unchangeable Chinese and the ever-changing Yankee brush against each other. And Europe here in her representatives shows herself superior to Mother Asia.

Farewell all to whom this will be welcome as a reminiscence of the past and beacon of the future.

/s/ John Banks

Pay Dirt
November 31—June 8

[The Buckeye Rovers and Meigs County Boys who stayed in the gold region at the close of the 1851 season found winter quarters at Ophir, where Banks and others had been working in the dry diggings. The next year they enjoyed some success at Ophir and nearby Gold Hill. With modest fortunes the last of the Buckeye Forty-Niners left California in June 1852.]

NOVEMBER 31: Tomorrow Logan leaves for home and I sent what I thought worthwhile up to this time.[1] Weather very fine. But [words missing] I have hurt my breast by lifting too hard. I feel aching but don't feel much uneasy as such. H[ope it will] wear away in a short time. James Gardner (crossed the plains with us) won, he says, nearly one thousand dollars at monte. He commenced by lending a gambler one dollar and fifty cents. No account of the mail of the middle [of the month] yet.

DECEMBER 7: Some rain last week, but not enough to cause the ravines to run. Mail for the middle and the first in Sacramento. Will probably get a letter by Wednesday or Thursday. This fall has been very healthy owing to the dry weather and the fact that but few emigrants arrived this season. A Mr. Hurd, of Michigan, has been lying sick in Drake's house nearly three months. His suffering has been great. Inflamatory rheumatism is the disease that afflicts him. His left arm and right leg have been lanced upwards of a quart of pus discharged from the latter. He is a mere skeleton but seems to be recovering. Hurd has a wife and eleven children. Says he owns considerable property. He is a man of considerable intelligence. He came here in 1849, and at present [has not] one cent. Friend Gardner broke and money [scarce].

DECEMBER 14: Read a letter from home. All well. [Words missing] past week very sore throat, and languor [words missing]. Worked the latter part of the week, feel [better] today. Weather keeps wonderfully dry. I [find] this dryer than last winter. Eighteen hundred and forty-nine must have been an uncommon year in California's history. Sold half our ditch and thrown up dirt for three hundred dollars, got only seventy-five dollars in hand. At present reading an English work entitled *Dialogues of Devils*. It contains some sound instruction well taught by their able Majesties. Each vice has its infernal advocates seeking to seduce Adam's children. I can see that many ideas are borrowed from Milton. But the work comes far short of *Paradise Lost*. An old number of the *Edinburgh Review* has fallen into my hands; contains some interesting matter. A review of Bishop Butler's work on the immortality of the soul is very beautiful. What wonderful beings we are from the profound philosopher looking almost around the compass to human vision, down to [word missing] thing in human form that is perfectly [words missing] not to see at all.

DECEMBER 21: Raining very fast. This is a sight for miners. It will enable them to wash gold, but sickness will be fearfully increased. There are but few miners here compared to what were here this time [last] year. I should judge the population of California also has suffered a sensible diminution. At present the greatest excitement is at Hangtown. Diggings are represented as being almost unparalleled; one pan of dirt contained nine hundred dollars. Quartz is again attracting some little attention again, but I think there is but little in this locality that will justify work at the present prices, which are normally five dollars per day, although a majority of miners are probably not making half. The Bear River ditch is dragging its slow length along.[2] The prospectors have not capital sufficient. They now say the work will be completed against May. The bull fight came off today. I did not leave home today. Those that saw it represent it as a cruel hoax, cruel to the steers (not bulls), and a hoax on the two dollar men.

Have been very hoarse all week, but cold much [better]. I could scarcely speak audible.

DECEMBER 28: Christmas again past and I from [home]. Time ever on the wing, it knows no rest. [Words missing] wake or sleep but time is bearing us to the [grave]. O Lord, to lay this body down! What an astonishing mystery is life and death. Death seems a [more] disturbable mystery than its mere forerunners. But what an incomprehensible idea is that of life. Ages of men passing away, millions rolling down the deep tide of time. Why we live, whence our power to think, how we move, what we [are], that Power that formed us alone can tell.

We live for happiness, yet what is happiness? What period in life was it in the past we did not then think so? Is the present joyous? No, but the future may be, and thus man is cheated out of his life, for the future, like a swift bird, takes good care to keep out of his way. We go on cheating from the cradle to the grave. But the best plan is not to think too much of that fair form called future pleasure, but to live on as good terms with this world as possible. Wrote home this week. [Word missing] again plagued by that affair called an express—no letter, though I almost know one is in the office for me. Present indications promise plenty of water. Rain almost [every day this] week. My cold rather better. Expect to work first thing next week.

JANUARY 4, 1852: I believe we would [not grow] old if we kept no account of [time], but figures are hard looking customers. . . . The yellow fever of New York is almost as fresh in [my memory] as [if it were] yesterday. We do not seem to think much [of health] or life, yet with what desperate fondness we cling to both. Millions of money for a mountain of time, and yet that precious commodity up to the moment sadly wasted. From the queen to the beggar we are alike. Last night I sat up with Mr. Hurd; he expired about three o'clock, having endured great suffering. His anxiety to live and hopes of recovery were manifest as long as reason held the reins, but the poor mortal was insensible some hours previous to his exit from this world. He scarcely spoke of death. Some time since I advised him, if he got able, to return home as speedily as possible, especially as he said he was the owner of considerable property. "No," said he with a terrible oath, "I will make a pile or leave my bones here." He had filled several places of public trust in Michigan. Today we bury him. He is decently laid out and will have a coffin. Two years since when hundreds were dying a blanket generally was a coffin and shroud, and the nearest place his grave.

Weather this week so that we worked nearly all the time.

Averaged about six dollars per day. A great many seeking employment by the day, more than I have seen at any previous time.

JANUARY 11: Wrote to Mrs. Hurd today. What sad [news] for a virtuous wife; the partner of her youth [who] left her in high hope can return no more. [Receive]d a letter from home. All well except [Uncl]e Robert. I feel very uneasy on his account as he is in the decline of life.[3] It is strange that an instrument of ten thousand strings can keep in tune so long. Very hoarse yet, and my pain in my breast troubles me. Great confusion on account of water. Several new ditches digging and everybody trying to get water, right or wrong. Our ditch out half the time.

JANUARY 18: Very unexpectedly another letter. All well. Saw Mr. Henderson of Athens.[4] Saw father and family a few days before he left. He says large numbers talk of coming here. They will rue the day. The Gold Hill boys are making money very fast. They made nearly an ounce per day last week. Three that came with Hurd hired by Reeves and Graham at seventy-five dollars per month and board. These chaps on Gold Hill have the water which is a cash article. Gardner's gave half an ounce per day for water for a sluice. Weather fine. Not making much. Health better.

JANUARY 25: Had a long talk with Henderson, he knows more of home affairs than any I have seen. Some of our old voyagers talk of coming back. Some of them told such yarns they want to leave: Steadman, twenty thousand dollars, lie enough for one man.[5] Best yet, beat that if you can. Drake don't tell. Well, if they deceive themselves, that is their fault. Wrote home today.

FEBRUARY 1: No rain yet. It is almost difficult to conceive of the strife for water. The oldest ditch claims all the surplus water in the ravine, and scarcely willing to leave enough in the ravine. The other ditches trying to get a little. The consequence is that sometimes there is not water sufficient for one Tom, though ten are working abreast. Up the miners come, shovel in hand, cutting ditches and swearing. "You must not cut mine; mine is the oldest, or mine is in the district." But they all get fair play, for all are cut. There has been two meetings held, but the end result is get water *if you can*. We are not in the muss as badly as others, our ditch is idle. We are working in a flue within a hundred yards of the ravine, but don't have water much more than half the time. Don't make much.

FEBRUARY 8: Weather yet fair. Bear River Ditch almost in. Working near our old claim when we made our first rise this week, made fifty dollars each. Last news from Europe, France is about exhibiting herself; Napoleon trying to run his uncle's race. Kossuth trying to get Jonathan into a scrape; he thinks Uncle Sam is big enough to fight. The Whigs trying to form a new platform, if not better than the last it won't sustain them long. Their war cry: "Union and the Constitution —and Office."

FEBRUARY 15: This evening received a most welcome and affectionate letter from home, dated January 1. All well. Graham going home in ten days, but I must stay longer.

A fight in Auburn, two said to be mortally wounded. Gambling the cause, though one of the sufferers, Mr. Smith, was passing and accidentally shot. Weather fine. Some doing very well. Gardner's making twenty to twenty-five dollars per day near Gold Hill.[6] Most of the men not making much.

Great strife about water and claims, as usual. This week made some five dollars per day. Sometimes the heat is very great for this season. I should think the sun as high as seventy some days.

FEBRUARY 22: Washington's birthday. Twenty years since this day I saw a most grand celebration, his centennial birthday. How little this season of the year here resembles that of any other place I have ever seen. Here we enjoy the bloom of flowers and the witching melody of birds. May in Ohio is not more balmy. I have seen neither snow nor ice, except once or twice a little ice in a vessel not thicker than window glass.

Today I spent in town waiting to see Graham, who is going home in the morning, but I left before he came. He is taking considerable money for others. He has done well this winter; he sold his share in the Gold Hill ditch for six hundred dollars, but it is not very profitable for the buyer at present as there is no water, and little or no prospect of any. Last week Ophir had a fire, two or three buildings destroyed. Here, where no insurance exists, fires are undoubtedly great calamities. California has some queer things; one for temperance men, milk fifty cents per quart, whiskey twenty cents. This looks favorable. Near where we work works an old Austrian. He is at work before daylight and last at night. A genuine miser, a kind of paste flour and water is his chief support. He is an old bachelor.

FEBRUARY 29: Some rain and great appearance of a protracted storm. March has been a bad, or good, month each year. Some have gone up in the mountains. They will not like this weather, while we in the dry diggings rejoice to see it. Some are making great wages down about Gold Hill. Gardner's work but little, yet make twenty-five to thirty dollars per day. Reeves and company average ten dollars per day and, if water comes, may make upwards of an ounce. Men are very willing to work at seventy-five dollars per month and many seeking employment. I am puzzled to know whether to go home this spring or not. I have done but little in the gold line. O now that I see many having a fair prospect of thousands, I feel as if to leave would be deserting at a bad time, but I hate to stay.

MARCH 7: Wild, stormy March—seems to be this month's true character. This is the third I have seen, and all stormy, but this exceeds both the former in the quantity of rain. Now the floods are tremendous. More rain has fallen in the last few days than for more than a year previous. Sacramento is a doomed city. Last night the American rose eighteen feet. Rain almost incessant. Provisions must rise. Those in the mountains have an awful time. Snow must be a very great depth. This is a very fair sample of 1849. Colds very prevalent. My throat sore. This month will in all probability be the only winter in this year. Every little ravine is a torrent.

MARCH 14: Done a foolish act, went to the circus. All the boys went and they teased me until I had to go. Price one dollar in the pit, two dollars in the box. A man by the name of Lee performed some most astonishing feats of agility. There were two English boys, aged some eight or nine years, surpassed anything I ever heard of. It would appear no animal possesses greater flexibility of body than man. I took a heavy cold in part pay; the evening was very wet and the tent leaked. A Texas Yankee by the name of Perry has bought up all the flour in town and raised the price from eight cents to twenty. Sacramento some six feet under water. Roads of course bad. No lack of water. Some miners doing amazingly well. We are making about six per day. A large lump in the Spanish Ravine, a few yards above where I worked last spring, weighs nearly seven ounces. Several others smaller, another not far off nearly one pound. The largest we have found this spring half an ounce.

MARCH 21: Weather delightful. Received a letter from Jane and Cornelius. Pretty good and it ought to be; they were some three or four months deliberating on the subject. No letter from home this mail. My mind is almost incessantly agitated about home. I am almost as much puzzled to know when I leave as I was whether to come at all or not. Steadman is here now, sick and out of money.[7] Those that left in company with him are scattered, all, as far as I may judge, badly disappointed. His big yarns has yielded a large but not a very good crop. Read of Athens in a Sacramento hospital deserted by all, but there penniless. He in all probability is now dead.[8] Sad news for his wife.

MARCH 28: Made nearly fifty dollars last week. Provisions down to their old price. Last night we had a little rain and it turned suddenly cold, almost as cold as any this month. This morning some ice. In other parts of the world it must be warm when rain falls; here our coldest weather is at a wet time. I hear passage home is very high. Many will go home by the plains. I judge passage much more than three hundred dollars. That is really too bad. Sometimes I think I must again try the plains. Wrote home.

APRIL 4: Weather very fine. The rush of men here is immense. Well-dressed men are now no scarcity. Miners generally making some four to six per day. Mining sometimes causes great strife, lawsuits common. A Mr. Peterson lost two hundred dollars by one trial about a ditch; this merely costs without lawyer's fees. We had an arbitration with some Irishmen about water. They beat, but unjustly I believe. I heard a witness demand his fee, five dollars. Oaths are very dear, yet extremely common. Two Georgians lost four thousand dollars, had it stolen this week.

APRIL 11: Three years from home. On Friday my mind was almost incessantly engaged in thinking of that day three years since. I cannot say, as I did a year ago this day, worth nothing, yet but very little taking the whole time into consideration. I have made over one thousand dollars in the last year. This week received a letter from home. All well. Dated February fourth, but mailed in New York the twenty-fourth. Sarah's letter is very neat in style, sentiment, and penmanship. Robert crazy to go West. Human beings seem to be near related to the wild goose, bird of passage.

APRIL 18: Heat very oppressive, almost equal to mid-summer. Ferrill has bought in with Giles. They are making about one hundred fifty dollars per week. They hire some hands. Giles told me he could get one hundred, if he wanted them. Very many hire from our part of Ohio. They look rather gloomy. Some that started from Panama three months since not heard from yet. E. Davis of our town here sick.[9] Some are making money fast. One lump of pure gold weighing thirty-two ounces, one of gold and quartz sixty-two, valued at five to six hundred dollars, yet another pure gold sixteen ounces. Many are turning their attention to farming, and raising stock of all kinds. A Dr. Wheatly has embarked in the hen speculation; he expects to keep some four hundred in laying order, price twenty-five to fifty cents per egg. Here is the old fable of the hen that laid golden eggs. Some of the gardens have strange enclosures, rawhide cut in strips and nailed twelve or eighteen inches apart much in use. Cows are becoming quite plentiful, though milk is yet fifty per quart.

APRIL 25: A little rain, weather rather cool. Could not get water. Tried a new place and made but little. Worked in the place and hired a hand, made twenty-five dollars. Ditches most all dry.

MAY 2: Received a letter from home. All well and very anxious for me to return. Bought one-eighth of Gardner's claim for two hundred fifty dollars. Gardner gone home. Joshua made twenty-two hundred dollars. We took out of the claim this week one hundred ounces and twelve dollars. Thursday we had nearly twenty-nine ounces, the largest day's work I have ever seen. It looked handsome in the pan. One is very apt to get excited. Gold seems no object, thus one day we forget the past. I feel more like staying.

MAY 9: Not quite so much this past week, made one hundred dollars. Water failing with us. Bear River Ditch is dragging its slow length along. Great excitement about claims. Some lawless fellows from the South are trying to jump claims. One arbitration where every man had a colt revolver. All kept cool. Great excitement about foreigners, especially Chinese who are arriving in the thousands and offering to work very low, some for board. The most cruel treatment is generally advised and will be resorted to, such as suffering no person to employ them and driving them back.

MAY 16: Most of the past week was cloudy, yet no rain. Wednesday evening about twenty men beat three or four Englishmen with stones. One is very badly bruised. Two brothers by the name of Clark. They are celebrated pugilists, but seem to be very civil men. I heard the oaths and distinctly heard several hard blows. Georgians were the aggressors. Today I climbed a tree to examine a hummingbird's nest. It is extremely beautiful. The nest is about half the size of a pigeon's egg. The eggs like white beans.

Passage considerably reduced, now $105 to New York.

JUNE 8: Steamship *Tennessee*.[10] What strange things crowd upon my mind. When I wrote the preceding, little did I think of going home. Now on the wide Pacific near Acapulco: Armstrong, Ferrill, Reeves, Giles, and myself.[11] All well. I left on the 29th instant for San Francisco. We embarked on this ship the 1st instant. Number of passengers four hundred and fifty; fare steerage ninety dollars.

Now in the torrid zone. Weather very warm. A few days and again in the midst of friends.

Epilogue

Athens County, observed a local editor in 1851, "has been as fully represented in the mines in the past three years as any other in Ohio, in proportion to her population." [1] "California fever" did indeed rage throughout the region during that time.

The Buckeye Rovers were but the first of several companies from Athens, Albany, Hebbardsville, and other towns. Many local residents made their way to *El Dorado* singly and in pairs. Two members of the original overland train—Steadman and Drake—inspired another large migration in the closing weeks of 1851; Steadman accompanied the adventurers and with the rest was temporarily stranded in Chagres when the transportation company defaulted on its obligation to provide passage to San Francisco. [2]

Armstrong, Banks, and their colleagues were more fortunate than many of the groups who subsequently started from Ohio in search of gold. They suffered no casualties from either disease or Indians en route to California, and only two losses—the Dixon brothers—while in the mining region. Also, they reached their destination at a time when opportunities for finding gold were still promising.

Those who worked on the Yuba or its tributaries found handsome fortunes which prompted their return to Ohio after one or two seasons. Others, including the diarists, did not find rich placers until 1851, or the following year, in Grass Valley. By June, 1852 all of the original Athens County Forty-Niners had left for home.

Many of the Ohio gold-seekers moved westward again with the flood of American migration in the years before the Civil War. At least two—Asa Condee and William Logan—returned to California. Harvey Graham was killed by Indians in the Black Hills. Banks, Elijah Ferrill, and George Reeves bought farms in Iowa where land was fertile and cheap.[3]

The Meigs County Boys, like their friends from Athens, returned to their homes by mid-1852. All but two of that group apparently remained in Rutland or adjacent communities. Alonzo Smith settled in Wisconsin, and James Gardner, the "best prospector and the most daring and reckless man" of the company, was killed in Nicaragua where he had joined a band of insurgents.[4]

Some of the Forty-Niners acquired wealth and prominent positions in the business or political life of Athens. William S. Wilson held many public offices, including that of mayor, probate judge, sheriff, and county treasurer. Soon after President Abraham Lincoln called for volunteers in 1861, he entered federal service as Captain of Company H, Thirty-Sixth Ohio Infantry, leaving the army four years later with the rank of Lieutenant Colonel.[5]

William S. Steadman became a successful building contractor and the operator of Athens's Steadman House, later the Hotel Palmer.[6] He died in 1899, shortly after Wilson's demise, leaving Armstrong the last of the Buckeye Rovers.

On returning to Hebbardsville Armstrong engaged in farming and the livestock business for many years before entering public service. In November, 1857 he married Lydia M. Carpenter of Meigs County; one child, J. Elza, Jr., died at the age of eighteen years.[7] Entering political life, Armstrong became a prominent leader of local Republicans, serving three successive terms, 1877–1879, as County Commissioner before winning appointment as Superintendent of the new Children's Home, east of Athens.[8] He held that position from 1883 until his death in 1905, and was succeeded by his wife.

On the homeward trip by way of Panama Banks fell victim to a tropical disease, perhaps malaria, which nearly proved fatal. Slowly over a period of many months he regained his strength; by mid-April of the following year he was well enough to turn attention once again to a diary. That which he considered a duty continued with many interruptions until his death forty-two years later. Those pages, he later mused, were part of a desire to live on in memory, a hope which was both natural and right.[9]

Farming was a hazardous occupation in 1853 as drought ravaged southern Ohio. Crops were disappointing, Banks noted, "wheat tolerably good, corn and oats very poor, grass light, and the streams nearly all dry." [10] The earth seemed charred by mid-summer, and late crops were total failures.

When the prospect did not improve the following season, Banks traveled by river steamer to the West in search of better land. The richness and beauty of south-central Iowa impressed him, as did the press of emigration; some five thousand, he estimated, had settled there in the previous year.[11] Near Knoxville, in Marion County, he purchased two hundred and sixty acres from the public domain, then returned to Ohio to dispose of holdings there, and to complete preparations for moving his family to their future home.

Later the same year he accompanied James Masheter, his

brother-in-law, and William Booth, a close friend, to Wisconsin to look for farming land. Finding prices too high they moved on to Iowa where all three purchased government land; Banks acquired another two hundred acres in Marion County.[12]

William and Mary Anne Banks with six of their grown children left Ohio in April, 1855, their third major move in America, to a final home on a farm along the Des Moines River in Clay Township, Marion County, Iowa. The elder Banks died six months later leaving John, the eldest son, as head of the family.[13] All of the children, except Jane Banks Inglefield and Hannah Banks Porter resided in or near Marion County for many years, maintaining the solidarity which had characterized the family since it had been planted in Ireland more than two centuries earlier.

Throughout a long and prosperous life John Banks retained those habits displayed so prominently in his overland and California diaries. In addition to keeping another record, his principal interests were religion and learning. A dissenter, he eventually rejected all churches because, in his view, the popular preachers did not accept Christ as the only hope for sinners—they were "trying to find some other way." [14] His ideas on gambling, dishonesty, violation of the Sabbath, and slavery never wavered.

In Ohio and in Iowa school teaching was a constant winter's task for almost twenty years. He conducted classes in small one-room schools and carried on the numerous chores of his farm, often commuting several miles in severe storms and icy blasts.

Reading was his favorite pastime, particularly on the Sabbath when there was time for not only the Scriptures, but also theology and history. Among the seven newspapers posted to the Banks home, Horace Greeley's *New York Tribune* was the best and received special attention.[15] Drawn to the Republican Party at an early date because of his attitude toward slavery, Banks remained loyal to that political faction until his death. In Republicanism he saw an instrument for establishing equality for former slaves and for denying power to Southerners who, in his eyes, remained forever unreconstructed.

At the age of forty-two years John Banks married a young lady of Danbury, Connecticut, with whom he had carried on a courtship by mail for about six months. In the fall of 1860 he went East hoping to find an "amiable and loving friend, a partner in life's joys and sorrows, and one to whom I might look for kindness and sympathy although all the world besides she might frown." Five months later he confided that Cynthia Adelia Judson had not disappointed him.[16]

Seven children—two girls and five boys—comprised the Banks family; all but one, Archibald Warren, lived to adulthood. John, a devoted father and loving husband, conveyed to his offspring the narrow standards of virtue and Christian faith by which he lived his own life. All were well educated by the standards of that time; three graduated from college, and even those who remained at home to work the farm shared their father's appreciation for learning and books. Clara, the oldest, devoted her life to teaching, and John Edwin worked for a Pittsburgh steel company as an engineer before taking up missionary work in Asia.[17]

A proud man, John taught his children to respect their family, both the living and dead. Their ancestors were honest and respectable, though seldom wealthy, nearly all farmers and intelligent. All were Protestants, usually of dissenting churches. Not one Banks had ever been in jail for debt or punishment for wrongdoing; none had betrayed a friend or had been deliberately false to any man.[18] According to tradition the family was noted for "intellectual ability and lack of common sense," which Clara Judson Banks interpreted to mean that her ancestors had been too honest to acquire riches and too generous to retain them.[19]

Two months after his seventy-seventh birthday, and more than forty-six years after the gold rush, John Banks succumbed to a final illness and old age. He was survived by his wife who lived another fifteen years, and by six children. John Edwin came into possession of his father's papers, including the diaries, and passed them on in turn to his children, to Wilma Banks Wagenblast and Edwin P. Banks, where they remain at the present time.

Both Armstrong and Banks looked back to their adventures in California with nostalgia which increased with the passing of the years. During one of his infrequent trips to Ohio Banks visited "Elzie" and William Wilson to talk of California times. On that occasion, thirty-seven years after the event, he observed that time had made old men of them all.[20] Three years later he expressed the wish to travel the overland trail once again, observing that what seemed like torture then was remembered almost with pleasure.[21] That sentiment was shared by Armstrong who later observed that although it was a hazardous undertaking, "we were all rather young and rather enjoyed it." [22]

The last survivors of the Buckeye Rovers—Banks, Armstrong, Steadman, and Wilson—reflected on their part in the gold rush with the certainty that they had been part of a grand drama in the panorama of American history. So wrote Banks in 1889:

Some of the events of the past had . . . an almost insignificant origin; Peter the Hermit arousing Europe, Columbus dreaming that the world must be round, and a little drunken man seeing a yellow spect in the mill race at Sutter's Mill. Yes, but the yellow spect was gold and now behold a nation sprung from it. Men from all parts of the earth moving toward it eager to catch the prize, we from Ohio swelling the crusade. Well, we did not get very rich, but we helped found an Empire: California, Oregon, and Washington, without mentioning Utah and her neighbors.[23]

Notes

INTRODUCTION

1 *The* (Columbus) *Ohio Statesman*, April 6, 1849. The best account of the impact of the gold rush on Ohio is Robert Thomas, "Buckeye Argonauts," *The Ohio State Archaeological and Historical Quarterly*, LIX (July, 1950), 256–269. This article is based on a chapter of an unpublished master's thesis, "The Impact of the California Gold Rush on Ohio and Ohioans" (1949), deposited in the Ohio State University Library.

2 The spread of "gold fever" in the eastern United States is discussed in Ralph P. Bieber, "California Gold Mania," *Mississippi Valley Historical Review*, XXXV (June, 1948), 3–28; *Southern Trails to California in 1849* (Glendale, California, 1937), 65–131.

3 *Gold Is the Cornerstone* (Berkeley and Los Angeles, 1948), 96.

4 Thomas, "Buckeye Argonauts," 256.

5 *U.S. Seventh Census: 1850* (Washington, 1853), xxxvi.

6 The movement of the Buckeye Rovers from Albany to Lexington is traced by Armstrong in sketchy notes in the front of his diary.

7 Georgia Willis Read and Ruth Gaines, eds., *Gold Rush: The Journals, Drawings, and Other Papers of J. Goldsborough Bruff, Captain, Washington City and California Mining Association, April 2, 1849–July 20, 1851* (2 vols., New York, 1944), I, 5, 438.

8 *Daily Cincinnati Gazette*, March 27, 1849.

9 Events on the trail and in California indicate that the Buckeye Rovers had a formal agreement providing for a common fund and mutual assistance. See for example Banks's entry for November 4, 1849.

[10] A(lonzo) Delano, *Life on the Plains and Among the Diggings* (Auburn and Buffalo, 1854), 117.

[11] George R. Stewart, *The California Trail: An Epic of Many Heroes* (New York, c.1962), 230–231.

[12] *Trail to California: The Overland Journal of Vincent Geiger and Wakeman Bryarly* (New Haven, 1945), 25.

[13] *Athens Messenger, and Hocking Valley Gazette*, July 5, 1850.

[14] A comprehensive bibliography for the Platte River route in 1849 appears in Dale L. Morgan, ed., *The Overland Diary of James A. Pritchard, from Kentucky to California in 1849* ([Denver], 1959), 177–200.

[15] *Ibid.* J. Elza Armstrong's diary is in The Ohio Archaeological and Historical Society, Columbus, the gift of Mr. John G. Keller, grandnephew of the writer, in 1949. John Edwin Banks's diary has been handed down two generations, and is now the possession of Mrs. Wilma Wagenblast and Mr. Edwin P. Banks, Denver, Colorado.

[16] *Centennial Atlas of Athens County* (Athens, 1905), 51.

[17] John Edwin Banks, "Memoirs." Typescript dated September 1, 1941 is in the possession of Edwin P. Banks.

[18] "Family Record" section of the Banks family Bible, in the possession of Edwin P. Banks.

1. LEXINGTON TO FORT KEARNY, *April 24—May 28*

[1] The Buckeye Rovers left St. Louis early on the morning of April 16 aboard the *Saluda*, which broke down en route to St. Joseph. By the time repairs were completed the channel had fallen to a level which prevented the steamboat from traveling beyond Camden; most of the passengers left the vessel at Lexington. See Read and Gaines, eds., *Gold Rush*, I, 5.

[2] Nearly fifty years after the event Armstrong recalled that his company joined a group from the Muskingum Valley to construct

a ferry on the Missouri four miles north of St. Joseph. See *Athens Messenger and Herald*, March 17, 1898. *Stryker's Magazine*, III (September, 1849), 58, placed Duncan's ferry four miles north of the city, but this was obviously an error for J. Goldsborough Bruff found it fifty-four miles to the north. Comparison of distances and landmarks noted by Armstrong and Banks with those of the diarists for the Charlestown (Virginia) Company, indicates that the Ohioans crossed the river at Savannah Landing (Amazonia), about thirteen miles above St. Joseph. See Read and Gaines, eds., *Gold Rush*, I, 446; Potter, ed., *Trail to California*, 35, 76–78.

3 At this point, approximately twenty-six miles northwest of St. Joseph, the Ohio train was on the Great Nemaha Reservation created in 1837 when the Iowa and the Sac and Fox tribes surrendered the "Platte Purchase" in western Missouri. The Presbyterians opened a mission and school on the reservation in 1837, and it was this which many emigrants visited twelve years later. See Pryor Plank, "The Iowa, Sac and Fox Mission and Its Missionaries, Rev. Samuel M. Irvin and Wife," Kansas State Historical Society *Transactions*, X (1908), 312–325.

4 Cholera was a constant threat to gold-seekers from the time they arrived on the Mississippi and Missouri rivers until they crossed the Rocky Mountains. One authority has concluded that because it "flourished in epidemic form on the Oregon-California trail, it would be hard indeed to arrive at an estimate of the fatalities resulting." See Georgia Willis Read, "Diseases, Drugs, and Doctors on the Oregon-California Trail in the Gold-Rush Years," *Missouri Historical Review*, XXVIII (April, 1940), 260.

5 The composition of the Ohio train is uncertain at this point, but it was typically mixed. In addition to thirteen men from Athens and ten from Meigs counties, there were Caleb Ferris of Michigan and W. H. Smith of Wisconsin, both of whom joined the train in St. Joseph. The Jenkins family included Thomas, his wife, and four children—two girls and two boys. The other three men in

the Jenkins party may have been Henry B. Lancaster, his son Henry, and John Chase. Jenkins (1801–1866) was a native of Dodgeville, Wisconsin and a veteran of the Black Hawk War. The title "General" appears to have been honorary since he served as a private in the Indian war; he was addressed as "Major" by residents of Dodgeville. *Athens Messenger and Herald,* March 17, 1898; Read and Gaines, eds., *Gold Rush,* I, 257; Milo M. Quaife, ed., *The Convention of 1846* (Madison, 1919), 780.

[6] This must have been part of the five companies of mounted riflemen who left Fort Leavenworth in early May for Fort Kearny, formerly called Fort Childs. The regiment had been recruited in 1846 for service on the Oregon Trail, but was diverted to the Southwest during the war with Mexico. At the close of hostilities it was reorganized and, in 1849, assigned to western outposts. See Raymond W. Settle, ed., *The March of the Mounted Riflemen: First United States Military Expedition to Travel the Full Length of the Oregon Trail from Fort Leavenworth to Fort Vancouver, May to October, 1849, as Recorded in the Journals of Major Osborne Cross and George Gibbs and the Official Report of Colonel Loring* (Glendale, California, 1940), 13–30, 35n.; Albert Watkins, "History of Fort Kearny," Nebraska State Historical Society *Collections,* XVI (1911), 235.

[7] For a description of the routes from St. Joseph and Independence to Marysville see Irene D. Paden, *In the Wake of the Prairie Schooner* (New York, 1943), 29–64; Stewart, *The California Trail,* 126–127.

[8] Banks is probably referring to one of the two companies which left Columbus in April. The Franklin California Mining Company, with thirty members, was under the leadership of Colonel Joseph Hunter; the Columbus Industrial Association, also thirty members strong, was led by J. Walton. *The* (Columbus) *Ohio Statesman,* April 3, 1849.

[9] The absence of Pawnees from the trail through Kansas was a matter of surprise and concern to many diarists. Perhaps the best

explanation was offered by Delano who stated that the tribe kept close to its villages and strongholds because of war with the Sioux. *Life on the Plains*, 48.

[10] Other diarists mentioned the fur-laden wagons that spring. James A. Pritchard, who was about ten days in advance of the Ohio train, encountered what may have been the same wagons west of Fort Kearny. See Morgan, ed., *The Overland Diary of James A. Pritchard, from Kentucky to California in 1849*, 67. The furs may have been from Fort Laramie, the American Fur Company's main depot on the North Platte. The role of that fort in the fur trade is discussed in LeRoy A. Hafen and Francis Marion Young, *Fort Laramie and the Pageant of the West, 1834–1890* (Glendale, California, 1938), 25–38, 44–94.

[11] Fort Kearny, established in 1846 where Table Creek emptied into the Missouri River, was moved two years later to a new location near Grand Island on the Platte. The name was changed from Fort Childs to Fort Kearny by a War Department Order dated December 30, 1848. Watkins, "History of Fort Kearny," 231–238, 241–243; Lyle E. Mantor, "Fort Kearny and the Westward Movement," *Nebraska History*, XXIX (September, 1948), 175–189.

2. FORT KEARNY TO SOUTH PASS, *May 29—July 5, 1849*

[1] The space devoted by diarists to the goods discarded along the trail west of Fort Kearny indicates that almost every emigrant wagon was overloaded at the start of the overland trip. Neither Armstrong nor Banks stated the weights of their wagons, but it is evident that they were also guilty of overloading, perhaps as the result of a desire to have provisions and equipment for any emergency in an unknown land. This may have been encouraged by some of the popular guidebooks. Joseph E. Ware, for example, advised that loads should not exceed 2,500 pounds, an excessive

weight. *Emigrant's Guide to California* (John Walton Caughey, ed., Princeton, New Jersey, 1932), 4–5.

[2] The high rate of accidents with firearms in 1849 was probably the consequence of the emigrants' fear of Indians, which prompted them to start overland heavily armed. For a discussion of arms and accidents see Potter, ed., *Trail to California*, 59–61.

[3] Ash Hollow, deriving its name from a scattering of trees found there, was the most convenient place to descend the bluffs on the south bank of the North Fork after crossing from the other branch of the Platte. A steep descent of from 400 to 500 feet, plus good water and grass, caused many emigrants to remember that place long afterwards. For a description of the valley see Edwin Bryant, *What I Saw in California* (New York, 1848), 97.

[4] *Ibid.*, 98. Bryant traveled overland to California in 1846 and published a guide which was widely used by gold-seekers. The popular guidebooks used in 1849 are discussed in Caughey, *Gold Is the Cornerstone*, 48–55.

[5] Names painted on wagons were noted by many diarists. See for example Delano, *Life on the Plains*, 71.

[6] Chimney and Courthouse rocks, unusual natural formations in what is now Morrill County, Nebraska, were favorite landmarks in 1849; almost every diarist mentioned one or both. Merrill J. Mattes, "Chimney Rock on the Oregon Trail," *Nebraska History*, XXXVI (March, 1955), 20–22; Earl R. Harris, "Courthouse and Jail Rocks: Landmarks on the Oregon Trail," *Nebraska History*, XLIII (March, 1962), 36–37.

[7] At this time Banks advanced his entries one day without interrupting the daily sequence. Sixteen months later he discovered and corrected the error.

[8] The bluffs were probably named for Hiram Scott, a fur trader who was taken ill and abandoned by his companions at that place in 1827 or the following year. Merrill J. Mattes, "Hiram Scott, Fur Trader," *Nebraska History*, XXVI (July-September, 1945), 127–162. An early version of Scott's story is in Bryant, *What I Saw in California*, 194.

9 Fort Laramie was sold to the United States in June, 1849 to serve as a military outpost on the overland trail. Hafen and Young, *Fort Laramie*, 139–143.

10 An abolitionist, Joshua Reed Giddings (1795–1864), was for twenty years a militant anti-slavery Congressman from Ohio's Western Reserve. Allen Johnson and Dumas Malone, eds., *Dictionary of American Biography* (20 vols., New York, 1928–1958), VII, 260–261. See also Eugene H. Roseboom and Francis P. Weisenburger, *A History of Ohio* (Columbus, 1953), 158, 162, 166–169.

11 Deer Creek crossing was the principal place where emigrant trains crossed the North Platte; the Mormon ferry was twenty-eight miles farther up river. Deaths by drowning at both places were exceptionally high in 1849. See Potter, ed., *Trail to California*, 111–112; Paden, *In the Wake of the Prairie Schooner*, 192–194.

12 This ferry was established in 1847 and maintained for five years by Mormons from Salt Lake. Dale L. Morgan, "The Mormon Ferry on the North Platte," *Annals of Wyoming*, XXI (July-October, 1949), 111–127.

13 Salaratus, or carbonate of soda, was common along the trail from the North Platte to the Sweetwater, and was frequently used by emigrants for baking bread in lieu of baking soda. Delano, *Life on the Plains*, 93; Paden, *In the Wake of the Prairie Schooner*, 206.

14 Willow Springs, approximately midway between the North Platte and the Sweetwater, possessed ample life-sustaining, non-alkaline water for man and beast. Paden, *In the Wake of the Prairie Schooner*, 203, 205–206.

15 Independence Rock, a spectacular natural formation on the bank of the Sweetwater, became the "great record of the desert" on whose massive base and towering sides thousands of emigrants bound for Oregon and California left their names. According to legend the rock acquired its name from a party of Oregon travelers, the first to travel overland by way of South Pass, who cele-

brated the Fourth of July at that place. Robert Spurrier Ellison, *Independence Rock: The Great Record of the Desert* (Casper, Wyoming, 1931), 7–8.

16 The deep, narrow gorge through which the Sweetwater passed to the North Platte excited the imaginations of many diarists and was a favorite landmark of the trail. See Paden, *In the Wake of the Prairie Schooner*, 213–214.

17 The "Ice Slough," a tributary of the Sweetwater, provided a pleasing novelty for Forty-Niners. Wakeman Bryarly, for example, joined officers of a government train in the enjoyment of mint juleps, an unfamiliar scene in the wilderness. Potter, ed., *Trail to California*, 119.

18 Edward Allen Hannegan (1807–1859), a Democrat, was appointed American Minister to Prussia on March 3, 1849. President James K. Polk gave the post to Hannegan, at the request of both Whigs and Democrats, after he failed to retain his Senate seat that year. The brother-in-law, whom Banks met on the trail, may have been Captain John R. Duncan of Newark, Ohio. Three years later Hannegan stabbed and killed Duncan during a drunken brawl in Covington, Indiana. See *Dictionary of American Biography*, VIII, 228–229; U.S. Department of State, *Register* (Washington, 1874), 93.

3. SOUTH PASS TO THE HUMBOLDT, *July 6—August 8*

1 James P. Vinyard, representative from Grant County, shot and killed C. P. Arndt, of Brown County, during debate on Governor James Duane Doty's nomination for the sheriff of Grant County. Indicted on the charge of manslaughter, Vinyard was acquitted on the grounds that he was defending himself from attack by the deceased. See Reuben Gold Thwaites, *Wisconsin: The Americanization of a French Settlement* (Boston and New York, 1908), 261; Moses M. Strong, comp., *History of the Territory of Wisconsin, from 1836 to 1848* (Madison, Wis., 1885), 381–385.

Charles Dickens cited this incident in his American Notes as typical of political life in the West. *Collected Works* (New York, 1888), VI, 443–444.

² Sublette's, or Greenwood's, Cutoff left the Oregon-California Trail between the Little and Big Sandy, and rejoined the route from Fort Bridger to Fort Hall near the present boundaries of Idaho, Utah, and Wyoming. Ware's *Emigrants' Guide to California* attributed the cutoff to Andrew W. Sublette; most diarists of 1849 accepted his word as accurate. Recent research indicates that the short cut may have been first traveled by William L. Sublette, one of the founders of Fort Laramie. See John E. Sunder, *Bill Sublette: Mountain Man* (Norman, c.1959), 92–99.

³ Odometers, or roadometers, were widely used by overland travelers for measuring distance. They were simple devices which, when actuated by a turning axle or wheel, indicated distance on the basis of the wheel's circumference, similar to the modern speedometer. See Read and Gaines, eds., *Gold Rush*, I, 437.

⁴ Because the Green River was unusually high and swift in 1849, fur trappers established a ferry at the trail crossing in the spring. This was taken over by Mormons from Salt Lake in June. It was impossible to ford the river safely for at least another two weeks after the Ohioans passed that point. Morgan, ed., *The Overland Diary of James A. Pritchard*, 156.

⁵ Banks saw the grave of Frederick Richard Fulkerson near Independence Rock, but recorded the year of his death as 1845, when the young man actually died July 1, 1847, thirteen days prior to his mother, who was buried near Green River. See Banks's entry for July 5. Correct dates were recorded by J. Goldsborough Bruff. See Read and Gaines, eds., *Gold Rush*, I, 54, 75.

⁶ Armstrong apparently repeated his entry for July 18. Thereafter his record corresponds with Banks, who was one day too fast.

⁷ Fort Hall, the northernmost settlement on the Oregon-California Trail, was established in 1834 by Nathaniel Wyeth, who later sold out to the Hudson's Bay Company. Its importance declined in late July, 1849, after the opening of Hudspeth's, or

Emigrant's, Cutoff which avoided the northern loop of the original trail to the Snake River. See Jennie Broughton Brown, *Fort Hall on the Oregon Trail: A Historical Study* (Caldwell, Idaho, 1932), 247–323.

8 The Jenkins family reached California in 1849, traveling the treacherous Lassen's Cutoff from the Humboldt to the northern mining region. J. Goldsborough Bruff encountered the family at his camp in the Sierra Nevadas on November 4, and related the tale of Jenkins's misfortune, as told by other emigrants. After leaving Bruff's camp with an ox and cart provided by people there, Jenkins received a mule and provisions from Major D. H. Rucker, in charge of relief for gold-seekers caught on the trail by early winter storms. Read and Gaines, eds., *Gold Rush*, I, 257–259, 619; D. H. Rucker, *Report, Sen. Exec. Docs.*, 31 Cong., 1 Sess., No. 52, 149.

9 It would appear that Banks refers to James Stewart, an experienced guide who led the "Diamond K Company" of Pittsburgh from Missouri to California in the record time of ninety-three days. Although Stewart passed through western Wyoming about that time, he and the Pittsburghers could not have been seen on that part of the Green River since they traveled the old trail to Fort Bridger and Salt Lake City. See Morgan, ed., *The Overland Diary of James A. Pritchard*, endpapers. A brief summary of Stewart's exploits is in Stewart, *The California Trail*, 229, 231, 249, 253, 265.

10 Delano described the Beer Springs in more precise terms: "At night we reached the first of the Beer Springs, two conical mounds, twenty feet high, with a base of more than a hundred feet in diameter, which was formed by the deposit of lime from the water." Delano, *Life on the Plains*, 137.

11 The cutoff was first traveled on July 19 by a company from Jackson County, Missouri, under the command of Benoni M. Hudspeth, with John J. Myers as guide. Both men hoped to find a direct route from the Bear to the Humboldt; the new route was

only a few miles shorter than the trail to Fort Hall and provided no appreciable savings in time. Morgan, ed., *The Overland Diary of James A. Pritchard*, 159–160. See also Stewart, *The California Trail*, 250–253.

[12] For some unknown reason Banks refers to the new trail blazed by Hudspeth and Myers as Lassen's Cutoff. Perhaps he confused this road with the cutoff opened the previous year by Peter Lassen from the lower Humboldt to the upper Sacramento Valley.

[13] Banks later revised his estimate of the distance saved by the cutoff (see his entry for July 31), but even then grossly exaggerated the value of the route. The actual gain was only about five miles. See Stewart, *The California Trail*, 135, 252–253.

[14] Daniel Dana, or Dane, apparently traveled alone the trail to California. Once in the mining region he joined Fall's Company of Cincinnati. *Athens Messenger, and Hocking Valley Gazette*, March 22, 1850.

[15] After leaving Goose Creek the California Trail turned southwest and crossed a divide to Thousand Springs Valley, better known as Warm or Hot Springs Valley in 1849. Two sub-basins were sometimes called Well Springs and Hot Springs Valley. Morgan, ed., *The Overland Diary of James A. Pritchard*, 163; Paden, *In the Wake of the Prairie Schooner*, 384–386.

[16] The Humboldt River rises in northeastern Nevada and follows a southwesterly course across a dry, barren land for about 350 miles before vanishing at the Sink. First called the Unknown River, it was later known as Ogden's, then Mary's, before John C. Frémont renamed it for Alexander von Humboldt, a famous German naturalist and traveler. Dale L. Morgan, *The Humboldt: Highroad of the West* (New York, c.1943), 5–6, *passim*.

4. THE HUMBOLDT TO CALIFORNIA, *August 9–September 20*

[1] Had this plan been carried out the Utes, who were responsible for raids on the emigrants' cattle, would have escaped punish-

ment; they invariably remained out of sight during the day when only the Diggers, a branch of the Shoshones, were seen on the road. See Potter, ed., *Trail to California,* 175n.

[2] A more detailed and different account of King's exploits appears in Delano, *Life on the Trail,* 214–215.

[3] Many gold-seekers followed the road from the Humboldt to the Feather River on the mistaken assumption that it was shorter than the two more popular routes by way of the Truckee and the Carson rivers. The northern trail was first used in 1846 by James Applegate on an eastward journey; two years later Peter Lassen led a train over the same route to the upper Sacramento Valley. The so-called cutoff was indeed the indirect one; many who labored over its desert wastes called it "Lassen's Horn Route." Ruby Johnson Swartzlow, "Peter Lassen, Northern California's Trail-Blazer," California Historical Society *Quarterly,* XVIII (December, 1939), 299–300; Stewart, *The California Trail,* 207–215, 297.

[4] Banks must have known that Hudspeth and Myers turned on to Lassen's Cutoff on August 20, five days before he reached that trail, and assumed that they were the first to take that route to Feather River. See Stewart, *The California Trail,* 223, 269–273.

[5] The Piutes form two separate divisions of the Shoshonean Indians of the Great Basin Region. Banks seems to be referring to what are called the true, or southern, tribe, close relatives of the Ute, who inhabited southwestern Utah, northwestern Arizona, and southern Nevada. See Frederick Webb Hodge, ed., *Handbook of American Indians North of Mexico,* Smithsonian Institution, Bureau of American Ethnology, *Bulletin* No. 30 (2 vols., Washington, 1910), II, 186–187.

[6] The Hot Springs, frequently called Boiling Springs, were the only natural source of water on the desert crossing, and one of the advantages of the Truckee route over the alternate trail to Carson River. See Paden, *In the Wake of the Prairie Schooner,* 430–431.

[7] The phrase "to see the elephant," meaning to gain experience

through hardship, or to suffer a particularly severe ordeal, was widely used by emigrants in 1849. William A. Craighe and James R. Hulbert, eds., *A Dictionary of American English* (4 vols., Chicago, 1938–1944), II, 874; Potter, ed., *Trail to California*, 187n. Elizabeth Margo insists that "seeing the elephant" became the slang of that day for traveling to California. *Taming the Forty-Niner* (New York, c.1955), 3.

[8] Salmon Trout was the name given by John C. Frémont to the river which the Murphy-Stevens-Townsend party of 1844 renamed Truckee in honor of the Indian who showed them the way across the uncharted Humboldt Desert and the Sierra Nevadas. Irene D. Paden, "Facts About the Blazing of the Gold Trail, Including a Few Never Before Published," *Pacific Historical Review*, XVIII (February, 1949), 5–6; Stewart, *The California Trail*, 69.

[9] The opening of the Truckee route is credited to Caleb Greenwood who guided, in 1844, the Steven-Townsend-Murphy party to California. Paden, *In the Wake of the Prairie Schooner*, 460.

[10] The Donner party, formed mainly of the Donner and Reed families from Illinois, was caught in the Sierra Nevadas by a blizzard in 1846; the survivors were finally rescued in the spring of the following year. Banks was familiar with Bryant's story of the group's hardship and suffering. A recent study of the tragedy is George R. Stewart, *Ordeal by Hunger: The Story of the Donner Party* (Cambridge, 1960), *passim*.

[11] Johnson's Ranch, established in 1846 by a New England sailor on the Bear River about forty miles north of Sutter's Fort, was the first place of habitation, other than mining camps, on leaving the Sierra Nevadas. For the early emigration it served as a sanctuary affording food and shelter for weary travelers. See Paden, *In the Wake of the Prairie Schooner*, 464, 470.

[12] At Steep Hollow the Ohioans entered the mining region. Claims had been worked there as early as June, 1848, and placers were still active when the overland emigration arrived the following year. Herbert Howe Bancroft, *History of California* (San Fran-

cisco, 1884–1890), VI, 355–356; Mahlon D. Fairchild, "Reminiscences of a Forty-Niner," California Historical Society *Quarterly*, XIII (March, 1934), 17–18.

5. CALIFORNIA, *September 21—February 3*

[1] James K. Polk, eleventh President of the United States, died on June 15, 1849, three months after leaving office, but not of cholera. Thomas Hart Benton, colorful U.S. Senator from Missouri, lived until April 10, 1858. See Allan Nevins, ed., *Polk: The Diary of a President, 1845–1849* (New York, 1929), 407n.; William Nisbet Chambers, *Old Bullion Benton: Senator from the New West* (Boston, c.1956), 439.

[2] Some gorges on the upper two forks of the American River were from 1,800 to 2,500 feet deep, with sides having an average slope of more than thirty degrees from bottom to top. Titus Fey Cronis, *The Natural Wealth of California* (San Francisco, 1868), 242. The Ohioans followed the crowd to that area. According to Bancroft, the "attention of new-comers continued throughout these early years to be directed toward the American River as the chief center and distributing point for mining movements." *History of California*, VI, 352.

[3] Deer Creek is a tributary of the Yuba River. Armstrong, Barnes, and Logan prospected in or near Nevada City until the start of the wet season, then moved to Vernon at the junction of the Sacramento and Feather rivers for the winter months. In a letter to an uncle, Armstrong insisted that they would have been better off had they stayed in the mines because provisions were high "and we did not have money to buy everything that we wanted." *Athens Messenger, and Hocking Valley Gazette*, July 5, 1850. See also *The Athens Messenger and Herald*, March 17, 1898.

[4] The sea routes and their hazards are discussed in Oscar Lewis, *Sea Routes to the Gold Fields: The Migration by Water to Cali-*

fornia in 1849–1859 (New York, 1949), *passim;* John E. Pomfret, ed., *California Gold Rush Voyages, 1848–1849: Three Original Narratives* (San Marino, California, 1954), 3–8.

[5] The Isthmus passage via Panama is discussed in John Haskell Kemble, "The Gold Rush by Panama, 1848–1851," Pacific *Historical Review,* XVIII (February, 1949), 45–56; *The Panama Route,* 1848–1869 (Berkeley and Los Angeles, 1943), *passim.*

[6] Cold Spring was located about half way between Coloma, on the South Fork of the American, and Hangtown (Placerville), on Weaver Creek.

[7] Weaver Creek, a tributary of the South Fork, yielded large fortunes in 1848 and 1849. Perhaps the richest placers were at Hangtown, later Placerville, where during the first year miners reportedly averaged from three ounces to five pounds of gold a day from dry diggings. Bancroft, *History of California,* VI, 74–75, 352–353. See also E. Gould Buffum, *Six Months in the Gold Mines: From a Journal of Three Years' Residence in Upper and Lower California, 1847–1849* (Ed. by John W. Caughey, 1959), 72–73.

[8] Charles M. Weber was one of the founders of the Stockton Mining Company, formed in the summer of 1848 to exploit dry diggings discovered at Hangtown. The stream was originally named for Weber, but became known in time as Weaver Creek, a corruption of the original. Bancroft, *History of California,* VI, 74; Buffum, *Six Months in the Gold Mines,* 76.

[9] The process of constitution-making and the provisions of that document are described in William H. Ellison, "Constitution Making in the Land of Gold," *Pacific Historical Review,* XVIII (August, 1949), 319–330. See also Bancroft, *History of California,* VI, 261–307.

[10] Peter Hardeman Burnett (1807–1895), a native of Tennessee, lived in Missouri before settling in Oregon in 1843. Attracted to California by gold, he found employment with John A. Sutter before gaining an appointment to the territorial courts. He played a prominent role in the movement for statehood and was elected

Governor on November 13, 1849, when the State Constitution was also approved. Johnson and Malone, eds., *Dictionary of American Biography*, III, 300–301.

[11] See Banks's entry for October 28, 1849. Different versions of the hangings which gave the community its name appear in G. B. Glasscock, *A Golden Highway: Scenes of History's Greatest Gold Rush, Yesterday and Today* (Indianapolis, c.1934), 62–63.

[12] One bloody campaign in 1849 resulted in the deaths of 175 Indians. John Walton Caughey, *California* (New York, c.1940), 381. Buffum describes the causes and consequences of the Indian troubles with some detail. *Six Months in the Gold Mines*, 80–81.

[13] The Chinese problem is discussed in Rodman W. Paul, "The Origin of the Chinese Issue in California," *Mississippi Valley Historical Review*, XXV (September, 1938), 181–196; Mary R. Coolidge, *Chinese Immigration* (New York, 1909), 15–40. See also Charles Howard Shinn, *Mining Camps: A Study in American Frontier Government* (New York, 1948), 203–204.

[14] Widespread feeling against Spanish-Americans and Latin-Americans may have been caused, at least in part, by hatreds engendered by the recent war with Mexico. Theodore H. Hittell, *History of California* (3 vols., San Francisco, 1885–1897), III, 263.

[15] Writing from Cold Spring, January 6, 1850, James C. Rathburn reported: "Charles and John S. Giles, with some Gallia County men, live near neighbors to us. I visit them, talk about the prospects ahead, and smoke together, all in harmony and in good cheer. They have reason to be in good cheer, for they make it when it does not rain from eight to twenty dollars per day. The other day Charles found a lump of gold worth $57. . . . Messrs. Paine, Stevens and Gardner have made about one ounce of gold ($16) per day, when they worked; others have not generally made so much. We are in the dry diggins. The rivers at this season of the year cannot be worked." *Athens Messenger, and Hocking Valley Gazette*, March 29, 1850.

[16] See Banks's entry for July 20, 1849 and footnote.

[17] This may have been one of three books: Percy Bolingbroke St. John, *The Trapper's Bride: A Tale of the Rocky Mountains* (2nd ed., London, 1845); J. S. Cummings, *Eolah: The White Flower of the Prairie! Or, The Trapper's Bride, a Story of Life in the Far West* (Boston, 1848), or Sir Charles Augustus Murray, *The Trapper's Bride; or, Spirit of Adventure* (Cincinnati, O., 1848).

[18] The size and variety of Banks's library reflects a life-long passion for learning. He later taught school in Ohio and Iowa until old age and failing sight forced his retirement. The early development of a book trade in California may account for the presence of literary and scholarly works in the mining camps. See Hugh Stanford Cheney Baker, "A History of the Book Trade in California, 1849–1859," California Historical Society *Quarterly*, XXX (June, 1951), 97–115.

[19] James Wilson Marshall (1810–1885), an Oregon emigrant in 1845, moved to California two years later. He was foreman for John A. Sutter, in charge of constructing a new mill on the South Fork of the American River when, in 1848, he found gold in the race. Caughey, *Gold Is the Cornerstone*, 6–8; Rodman W. Paul, *California Gold: The Beginning of Mining in the Far West* (Cambridge, 1947), 16–17.

6. THE AMERICAN RIVER, *February 10—August 11*

[1] Middle Fork was called the richest of the three branches of the American River. In June, 1848 a party of Mormons opened the first placer on that stream at Spanish Bar, from which more than a million dollars was eventually taken. There were more bars on the Middle Fork than on any other watercourse in the mining region; many yielded from one to three million dollars each. Bancroft, *History of California*, VI, 73, 354.

2 Sacramento, at the junction of the Sacramento and American rivers, became the principal commercial center for the northern mines. Delano, who visited the city in March, 1850, was also impressed with its rapid growth. *Life on the Plains*, 288–289.

3 President Zachary Taylor's "First Annual Message to Congress," December 4, 1849, noted that California had commenced work on a constitution and recommended that its application for statehood receive favorable action from the legislators. He also cautioned that body against interjecting sectional issues into the question of admission to the Union. James D. Richardson, ed., *Messages and Papers of the Presidents* (10 vols., Washington, 1903), V, 18–19.

4 Walker's six letters probably refers to the publications of John Walker (1768–1833), founder of the Church of God in Dublin, Ireland. Walker's followers were called "Separatists," or "Walkerites." Banks may have been reading Walker's *Letters to Alexander Knox* (Dublin, 1803). See "John Walker" in *The Dictionary of National Biography* (22 vols., London: Oxford University Press, 1917, 1973), XX: 534. John Banks, as well as his parents and siblings, was a Separatist. It seems likely that the middle name of John's brother, James Walker, was in honor of John Walker.

5 William Booth was a close friend with whom Banks traveled, in 1854, to Iowa to purchase land for his future home. See Banks's Diary, December 3, 1854.

6 A more detailed description of gambling houses in Sacramento is in Delano, *Life on the Plains*, 289.

7 Circumstances forced the mining camps to establish some form of local government. The majority resorted to the alcalde, similar to that institution once prominent in Spain's North American empire. The alcalde was usually given power to record claims, settle disputes, and to enforce civil and criminal law. Shinn, *Mining Camps*, 174–178.

8 Jane, two years younger than John, married Cornelius Inglefield. No date is given for this union in the Banks family Bible,

in the possession of Mrs. Wilma Wagenblast, Denver, Colorado.
9 At least one effort was made to attract respectable American ladies to the mining regions. Lewis, *Sea Routes to the Gold Fields*, 34–41.
10 The race, if Banks used the term correctly, was an artificial channel for diverting water from a stream to a claim for washing gold-laden dirt. Since he later reported that the race had grown to 100 feet (June 28), and then to 480 feet (August 11), it probably was a sluice; that is, a series of troughs in the bottom of which riffle bars caught the gold as water carried away dirt and debris. The sluice, a modification of the Long Tom, reduced the cost of washing while extracting a larger proportion of gold from dirt. Bancroft, *History of California*, VI, 410–411; Paul, *California Gold*, 62–63.
11 Earheart and Dewing must have completed a fast passage to the mining regions during the winter of 1849–1850, as indicated by the fact that they brought letters from families of the Buckeye Rovers. They probably traveled by way of Panama.
12 The disappointment experienced by newcomers was revealed by O. H. Chapman who went overland to California, writing from Weavertown, August 10, 1850. ". . . We are in California—and, what are the prospects, I suppose you would inquire. Well, to tell the plain truth, this year's emigration are sadly humbugged. . . . I should say that the best mining days for California are over. Every creek and ravine in this part of the country has been explored, and in a measure dug out, and I am informed such is the case all over the country; and the only places where gold has been found in sufficient quantities to pay, are in ravines, and creeks and rivers. I am told that on the largest streams—the Yuba, South and Middle Fork, Bear River, etc.—every foot of ground is occupied by claims, and there are thousands there who can't get a chance to dig at all." Reprinted from the Meigs County *Telegraph* in the *Athens Messenger, and Hocking Valley Gazette*, October 25, 1850.
13 The Gold Lake rumor drew many miners to the northern min-

ing district and, although unfounded, greatly accelerated exploration on the headwaters of the Feather River. One miner learned that Gold Lake was so rich that "out of every 9 pans of dirt you wash a man is sure to have 7 of them with 2 oz. each." Charles L. Camp, ed., "An Irishman in the Gold Rush—The Journal of Thomas Kerr," California Historical Society *Quarterly*, VIII (June, 1929), 24.

7. OPHIR, *August 18—February 20*

[1] Salmon Falls, one of the mining centers opened on the South Fork of the American in 1849, was organized as a town the following year, and had at one time a population of 3,000, sustained by such nearby camps as Pinchemtight, Jayhawk, Green Springs, and McDowell Hill. Bancroft, *History of California*, VI, 352.

[2] Bancroft has developed this thesis, showing that in 1852 "the average yield for each of the 100,000 men engaged in mining was only $600, or barely $2 per day, while wages for common labor ruled twice and three times higher." Furthermore, if the profits of employers and a few fortunate ones were excluded, the average fell to not more than $1 a day. *Ibid.*, 423–424.

[3] Shirt-Tail Canyon was located on the narrow divide between the Middle and North Forks of the American, and ranked with Yankee Jim's, Todd's Valley, Wisconsin Hill, and Iowa Hill as an important mining center. *Ibid.*, 73, 355.

[4] Murderer's Bar on Middle Fork derived its name from a massacre of five miners by Indians in 1849. *Ibid.*, 354. See also Owen C. Coy, *In the Diggings in 'Forty-Nine* (Los Angeles, 1948), 34, 36–37.

[5] Zachary Taylor, twelfth President of the United States, died of acute gastroenteritis on July 9, 1850. See Holman Hamilton, *Zachary Taylor: Soldier in the White House* (Indianapolis and New York, c.1951), 388–393.

[6] These men were probably from Rutland or Pomeroy; companies were organized in each town for the overland journey in 1850.

NOTES / 219

Athens Messenger, and Hocking Valley Gazette, March 1, 1850.
7 The Rich Dry Diggings, or North Fork Dry Diggings, discovered in 1848, became the town of Auburn a year later, and the seat of government for Placer County. Bancroft, *History of California*, VI, 73; Coy, *In the Diggings in 'Forty-Nine*, 13.
8 Wilson and Condee reached Athens in late November, 1850, at which time the local newspaper observed, "they secured a very respectable pile." *Athens Messenger, and Hocking Valley Gazette*, November 29, 1850.
9 Ophir, located in the midst of dry diggings, was originally named Spanish Corral. Giles renamed the settlement for the source of King Solomon's fabulous treasure. For a brief time in the early 1850's it was the largest community in Placer County. Bancroft, *History of California*, VI, 355n.
10 The cost of passage between San Francisco and New York, via Panama, fluctuated in proportion to the competition between the government-subsidized mail lines and the so-called "independents." Although Banks thought the fare prohibitive in 1850, it was in fact less than half what it had been the previous year. See Kemble, *The Panama Route, passim*.
11 At this time Banks corrected an error made on June 13, 1849 when he advanced the dates of his entries by one day.
12 An abolitionist, Banks viewed the Compromise as a triumph for the South, even though by its terms California was admitted to the Union as a free state. The issue of slavery expansion and the struggle over the Compromise are fully treated in Allan Nevins, *Ordeal of the Union* (2 vols., New York, 1947), I, 253–345.
13 Gold Bluff, located on the Pacific between Trinidad Bay and the mouth of Klamath River, was the scene of an important rush after fine particles of gold were discovered in the sands along the beach. The excitement over finding washed gold was short-lived, however, for miners found there was no economical method for separating the fine metal from the sand. Bancroft, *History of California*, VI, 394; Coy, *In the Diggings in 'Forty-Nine*, 85.

¹⁴ The abortive Gold Bluff rush of 1850–1851 and prospecting by gold-seekers from Oregon opened the mines of the Klamath River and its tributaries. Scott River became known for its coarse gold and nuggets. Scott Bar, near the junction of the Scott and Klamath rivers, was perhaps the most famous camp; others included Junction, Slapjack, Lytte, Poorman, French, and Johnson bars. Bancroft, *History of California*, VI, 365–367.

¹⁵ Most of the bars were on the American River: Rattlesnake and Condemned on the South Fork; Murderer's on Middle Fork; and Rich on the North Fork. Stony Bar was on the Yuba, and there was also a Murderer's Bar on the Klamath. Coy, *In the Diggings in 'Forty-Nine*, 34, 60–61, 88.

8. AUBURN-OPHIR, *February 23—November 23, 1851*

¹ The first segment of the diary was delivered to the Banks family by Earheart on his return to Athens, probably in the spring of 1851.

² The Coyote Diggings, better known as Coyoteville, were in Nevada County, immediately northwest of Nevada City. Discovered in May, 1850, the diggings were named for the method of mining, or burrowing, also called "coyoteing." There were also Coyote Diggings in Plumas and Tuolumne counties. Erwin G. Gudde, *Cailfornia Gold Camps: A Geographical and Historical Dictionary of Camps, Towns, and Localities Where Gold Was Found and Mined; Way Stations and Trading Centers*. Elisabeth K. Gudde, ed. (Berkeley: University of California Press, 1975), 86–7.

³ Hubert Howe Bancroft discusses the development of canals and ditches on Deer and Rock creeks in *History of California*, VI, 413–414. Deer and Rock creeks are identified in Gudde, *California Gold Camps*, 93, 294.

⁴ Grass Valley became an early center for mining of goldbearing quartz or auriferous ores, in 1850–1851. The "principal machine," to which Banks refers, was a stamp mill. Bancroft states that the

first stamp mill in California was operated at Grass Valley in the summer of 1851, and that it inaugurated a new era of mining in the state. *History of California*, VI, 356.

5 Henry Hastings Sibley (1811–1891) was a "free soiler," a delegate to the U. S. Congress from Wisconsin Territory in 1848, and the first Governor of the State of Minnesota, 1858–1860. Wendell Phillips (1811–1884), famed orator and reformer, dedicated most of his life to the cause of abolition.

6 Rough and Ready was in Nevada County, about seven miles southwest of Nevada City. The rich placer mines were exhausted by the mid-1850s. Gudde, *California Gold Camps*, 297.

7 Onion Valley was located in Plumas County at the head of a tributary of the Middle Fork of Feather River. At the time gold was discovered there in 1850, the valley contained an abundance of wild onions, for which it was named. Ibid., 251–2.

8 Here Banks refers to the Separatist leader, John Walker, founder of the Church of God. Morgan and Mansel may have been theologians, if not subordinates in the Separatist movement. See "John Walker," in *The Dictionary of National Biography* XX: 534.

9 Phrenology, a theory that the shape of the skull revealed evidence of human character traits and mental powers, was developed in the early nineteenth century by Franz Joseph Gall, a German physiologist, and others. The new "science" of phrenology was popularized in the United States and abroad by Orson and Lorenzo Fowler. Fowlerism, a widely accepted philosophy that extolled individualism and adherence to moral law, reached the peak of its popularity in the 1840s and 1850s. By the twentieth century it was generally viewed as a form of quackery. John D. Davies, *Phrenology, Fad and Science: A 19th-Century American Crusade* (New Haven: Yale University Press, 1955), passim.

10 Francois Marie Charles Fourier (1772–1837), a French philosopher and reformer, was translated and popularized by Albert Brisbane (1809–1890), a journalist, in Horace Greeley's New York *Weekly Tribune*. Fourier rejected the constraints imposed

by society on individuals in favor of the free development of human passions, of which he identified twelve. Phalanges founded in the United States in the 1840s and 1850s were modeled on Fourier's teachings. See Everett Webber, *Escape to Utopia: The Communal Movements in America* (New York: Hastings House Publishers, 1959), 184–199.

[11] The tale of Dick Whittington and his cat had its origin in an early seventeenth-century English play, which was subsequently lost. According to the play, Whittington, an orphan kitchen boy, became rich when the ruler of Morocco purchased his cat for a large sum of money because the kingdom was overrun with rats. Richard Whittington (1358–1423), a London merchant and lord mayor of the city, is mistakenly thought to have been the Dick Whittington of the fable.

[12] Braintree, a suburb of Boston, was the birthplace of John Adams and John Hancock. Quincy split off from Braintree in 1792, and was incorporated as a city in 1888.

[13] A fire destroyed approximately three-fourths of San Francisco in May, 1851.

[14] "What news from Sydney?" appears to be a reference to the criminal element in the gold regions. "Sydney-duck" was used to identify the large number of Australians, many of them of disreputable character, who joined the rush to California in 1849 and following years. Eric Partridge, *A Dictionary of Slang and Unconventional English* (7th ed., New York: The Macmillan Company, 1970), 1449. See also Gudde, *California Gold Camps*, 319.

[15] The activities of Chinese miners in California are discussed in Rodman W. Paul, "The Origin of the Chinese Issue in California," *Mississippi Valley Historical Review* XXV (September, 1938), 181–196. See also Gudde, *California Gold Camps*, 71–2.

[16] Nelson Creek was a tributary of the Middle Fork of Feather River. The diggings were very rich and at the height of develop-

ment in the summer of 1851. Gudde, *California Gold Camps*, 236–7.

[17] Shirt Tail Canyon was in Placer County. Some of the Buckeye Rovers had been there in August, 1850. Also in Placer County was Bird's Valley, where auriferous ore was mined. The underground workings may have prompted Banks's use of the term "Coyote." Ibid., 38, 318. Potosi was the Bolivian community that supplied most of the world's silver in the late sixteenth century.

[18] Todd's Valley, Placer County, was on the Middle Fork of the American River. Ibid., 351.

[19] On at least five different occasions, Banks mentioned Green Buler, or Beeler, who was from Missouri. Banks's handwriting is sometimes illegible, or nearly so. If the former spelling is correct, it may have been shorthand for Buehler.

[20] There were two Horseshoe Bars, one on the North Fork of the American River below Auburn, the other above the city on the Middle Fork of the American, about five miles south of Bird's Valley. Banks refers here to the lower site. Ibid., 160.

[21] Banks is reacting to reports that General Narciso Lopez's filibuster expedition against Spanish rule in Cuba had failed, and that Lopez, with many of his forces, had been executed. Lopez has been a controversial figure in Cuban historiography. Some historians view him as a martyr in the struggle for Cuban independence; others, perhaps a majority, insist that he sought nothing more than the annexation of Cuba as a slave state by the United States. Basil Rauch, *American Interest in Cuba, 1848–1855* (New York: Columbia University Press, 1948), 121–80; and Philip S. Foner, *A History of Cuba and Its Relations with the United States*: Vol. 2, 1845–1895 (New York: International Press, 1963), 41–60.

[22] The Secret Diggings, also called Secret Canyon, were about ten miles from Nevada City. Gudde, *California Gold Camps*, 314.

9. PAY DIRT, *November 31—June* 8

[1] Bank's second diary, for the period from February 23 to November 23, 1851, was sent home by William Logan, but if it reached Albany, and there is no evidence to indicate that it did, the family lost it in later years.

[2] Placer County had twenty-nine canals, or ditches, in 1855, the largest of which was the Auburn and Bear River Water Company's waterway with a main line fifty miles long and branches aggregating 150 miles. Bancroft, *History of California*, VI, 356.

[3] Robert Banks died August 10, 1852, a few weeks after John Banks returned to Albany. He described his uncle as "my constant companion and beloved friend from earliest childhood." Diary, August 11, 1852.

[4] Alexander Henderson, a farmer from Athens County, left for California in December, 1851, traveling by way of the Isthmus. *Athens Messenger, and Hocking Valley Gazette*, December 26, 1851.

[5] Steadman, who with Denis Drake returned to Athens in October, 1851, returned to the gold regions with thirty or forty men (and one woman) from Alexander and Lee Townships. That party sailed from New York on December 29 aboard the *Independence* for Panama. *Ibid.*

[6] There were at least three different mining communities named Gold Hill. One was near Placerville, another was in Grass Valley in the vicinity of Nevada City, and the third was west of Auburn and Ophir. It was at the last place that Banks spent the final months of his stay in California. Until the "missing" segment of the diary was found, it appeared, from sketchy internal evidence, that Banks had relocated to the northern-most Gold Hill near Nevada City. This was an error.

[7] The gold-seekers who sailed from New York in late 1851 experienced unexpected delay and hardship en route to California. On reaching Panama City some of the group published a warning to emigrants about the treatment they had received from Edward

Mills, operator of vessels in the New York-Chagres trade. The complaint stated that passengers had purchased tickets to San Francisco, but because the *Independence* was not seaworthy they were forced to buy passage on another ship from Jamaica to Panama, where they were stranded without hope of completing the trip on their original tickets. The Ohioans were far more fortunate than they realized, for the *Independence*, after leaving Kingston, was never seen again. *Athens Messenger, and Hocking Valley Gazette*, February 27, 1852; Kemble, *The Panama Route, 1848–1869*, 321.

8 Isaac Reed, one of the party temporarily stranded in Panama, died in Sacramento on March 20, 1852. A bootmaker by trade, he had been suffering from an illness for two years, a condition from which he sought relief in California's warm climate. *Athens Messenger, and Hocking Valley Gazette*, May 14, 1852.

9 This may have been John Davis, a farmer, who sailed from New York with the Athens County group in December, 1851. *Ibid.*, December 26, 1851.

10 The *Tennessee* was a wooden side-wheel steamer of 1,275 tons burden employed by the Pacific Mail Steamship Company on regular schedules between San Francisco and Panama. Less than a year after Banks traveled on that ship it went aground in Bolinas Bay, four miles north of the entrance to San Francisco Bay, and was demolished. Kemble, *The Panama Route, 1848–1869*, 248.

11 Banks and his companions reached Athens in about forty-five days, a quick trip compared to the overland journey three years earlier. *Athens Messenger, and Hocking Valley Gazette*, July 16, 1852.

EPILOGUE

1 *Athens Messenger, and Hocking Valley Gazette*, November 14, 1851.

2 *Ibid.*, November 28, December 26, 1851, February 27, 1852.

3 *The Athens Messenger and Herald*, March 17, 1898.

4 *Ibid.*

5 A. H. Mattox, comp. and ed., *The Athens Home Coming Reunion, June Fourteenth, 1904* (New York, 1904).

6 *Ibid.; The Athens Messenger and Herald*, October 19, 1899.

7 *Centennial Atlas of Athens County*, 51.

8 The Athens County Children's Home was authorized by an act of the Ohio Legislature in 1880, following a public subscription which raised $12,000 for that purpose. The County Commissioners purchased 125 acres one mile east of Athens in 1880, and the main building was completed the following year. See *History of Hocking Valley, Ohio* (Chicago, 1883), 222–223.

9 Banks's Diary, October 9, 1891.

10 *Ibid.*, July 2, 1853.

11 *Ibid.*, July 11, 1854.

12 *Ibid.*, December 3, 1854.

13 "Family Record" section, Banks family Bible.

14 Banks's Diary, September 18, 1870.

15 *Ibid.*, September 13, 1868.

16 *Ibid.*, May 20, 1861.

17 Memoirs of John Edwin Banks, September 1, 1941.

18 Banks's Diary, September 18, 1870.

19 Memoirs of John Edwin Banks, September 1, 1941.

20 Banks's Diary, August 25, 1886.

21 *Ibid.*, April 9, 1889.

22 *The Athens Messenger and Herald*, March 17, 1898.

23 Banks's Diary, April 9, 1889.

Index

Deer Creek Crossing, Platte River, 205 (fn 11)
Dentist, 139; pulling teeth, 165
Des Moines River, 194
Devil's Gate, xv, 28–29, 206 (fn 16)
Devil's Peak, 86–87
Dewing, Isaac, 123–126, 129, 137, 144, 147, 152, 217 (fn 11)
Diamond K Co., Pittsburgh, Pennsylvania, 208 (fn 9)
disease, sickness, 20, 40, 87, 93, 94, 97; cholera, 6–7, 10, 20, 36, 38, 91, 142–144, 146, 201 (fn 4); cold, 107, 111–113; consumption, 152; dysentery, 136; epilepsy, 143; erysipelas, 156; exposure and fatigue, 111; faint, 108; gastric disorder, 107; inflammatory rheumatism, 179–180; malaria, 196; scurvy, 110; smallpox, 6, 38; strangury, 77
Dixon, Dr. Joseph D., xii, xiv–xv, 4, 53, 58, 191; death of, 96; grave of, 98.
Dixon, Hugh, xii, 4, 96, 99, 104, 111, 140, 191; death of, 142
Donner cabins, 85, 87
Donner Party, 85, 211 (fn 10)
Drake, Denis, xii, 24, 91, 102, 104, 107, 112–113, 117, 119, 121, 123, 125, 135, 141, 147–148, 165, 169, 179, 183, 191, 224 (fn 5)
drugs: calomel, 107; laudanum, 143; opium, 136
drunkenness, xxii, 6–7, 16, 36, 40–41, 115, 125, 132, 141–142, 146, 152–153, 159, 162, 164, 167, 170–171, 173–174
Dry Sandy, 36
Duckett, Kenneth W., v
Duncan, John R., 206 (fn 18)
Duncan's ferry, Missouri River, 200–201 (fn 2)

Dunn, of Illinois, 20
Dutchman, 156

Earheart, John, 123–124, 126, 139–140, 142; tending to sick, 143–145; prospecting on Bear River, 147–148, 217 (fn 11); carrying home segment of Banks's diary, 149–151, 220 (fn 1)
Edmonds, "Keeper of the Tombs," 78
El Dorado, xi
Eldorado Canyon, 120–122, 124, 126, 131, 135
Eldorado County, California, 141
"elephant, see the," 77, 86, 210–11 (fn 7)
Ellis, 155
Emigrant's Cutoff, xv, 208 (fn 7)
Englishman, 189–190
Enscoe, Dr., 156
Esmond, 128
Estell, 33
Everette, 31, 38

Fall River, 151
Feather River, xvi, 73–74, 95, 128, 133–134, 148, 151–152, 162–163, 212 (fn 3); cutoff to, 71
Ferrill, Elijah, xii, xvii, 73, 99, 111, 139, 144, 147, 162, 173, 175, 188, 190, 192
Ferris, Caleb, xiv, 71, 201 (fn 5)
ferry, construction of by Buckeye Rovers, Missouri River, 200–201 (fn 2)
fighting, 159, 162
filibusters, 171, 223 (fn 21)
fires, 153, 185
fishing, 69; fishing pole, 84
flora: wildflowers, 185; buffalo berry, 72–73; bulrush, 70; cedar, 21–22, 28, 88, 94, 125; clover, red, 62; corn, 4; cottonwood, 22,

A Note about the Authors

H. Lee Scamehorn is Professor of History at the University of Colorado, Boulder campus.

Edwin P. Banks is the grandson and Jamie Lytle-Webb is the great-granddaughter of diarist John Banks.